CW00340836

Plant-Based Air Fryer Cookbook for Beginners

Affordable, Easy & Delicious Plant-Based Air Fryer Recipes to Heal Your Body & Live A Healthy Lifestyle (21-Day Meal Plan)

Kelly Bentrin

Table of contents

Introduction

In this modern age, we have found out the formula for a healthier and fulfilling life. Doing exercise, being less stressful, and, most importantly, eating right. Scientific research has shown us that consuming more plant products and reducing meats, processed, and fast foods from our plate will drastically decrease our chances of being infected or stricken by some chronic disease. It is gaining popularity by the second with people of every spectrum diving into this new and beneficial fad. You may know of someone vegetarian or pescatarian, but no matter what type of plant-based diet the person is on, the main objective is to cut down on meat, sugar, and fat.

Read on to know more about how a plant-based diet will bring you back on track of a healthy diet.

Chapter 1: Understanding the Plant-Based Diet

What Is A Plant-Based Diet?

There is no set definition of a plant-based diet, but it generally means to shift eating habits by adding more fruits, vegetables, legumes, nuts, and whole grains in your diet. Someone new to this topic might confuse the plant-based diet as a diet that completely cuts off other items such as meat, but that is not the case. It should be looked upon as a diet that discourages rather than strictly prohibits the use of animal and processed products. Each individual can opt for their preference for a plant-based diet according to their goals and ability of self-control.

There are different types of plant-based diets which include:

Flexitarian: In this diet, the person does eat some meat and dairy but focuses mainly on plant-based products.

Pescatarian: These people do not eat red meat but consume seafood, eggs, and other dairy products.

Ovo-vegetarian: The people following this diet do not eat poultry, red meat, seafood, or any dairy products but do consume eggs.

Lacto-vegetarian: These people eat dairy but exclude from their diet eggs, red meat, and seafood.

Lacto-Ovo vegetarian: People that consume eggs and dairy products but not red meat, poultry, and seafood.

Vegans: It is the strictest form of this diet in which the person does not eat any animal-based product, including eggs, dairy, and honey. They need to see labels and other details in whatever they buy and consume carefully.

Benefits of Plant-Based Diet

The plant-based diet has become a fad all around the world and is even preached on social media because of the vast amount of benefits they provide. Despite stereotypes, it isn't just a way to make yourself seem better to others; on the contrary, people following this lifestyle are more caring and self-aware than other people. They know that the benefits of this diet range from increased mortality to saving the planet. Some benefits include:

- Losing weight

Obesity and its associated problems have gripped the Western world. A study showed that in the USA, 69% of the population suffer from obesity. With fast foods readily available and every food package filled with sugar, these numbers show the consequences of not looking after what you eat.

Losing weight should not be pursued to just look good, but also to live a better life free of diseases. Eating a diet rich in fiber and mainly plant-based helps to maintain a steady weight for a long time. Only by excluding animal-based products and processed food, a lot of improvements can be seen in a few months.

- Save guards from several diseases

Chronic diseases that are responsible for the deaths of millions of people each year like hypertension, diabetes, etc., can be controlled and prevented by following this diet. Many forms of cancers, in recent studies, have been shown to affect people less who are following plant-based diets. Cognitive diseases like Alzheimers and Parkinson's have also shown to less likely affect dieters because it slows the progression of these diseases.

- Saving the planet

Global warming is a real and urgent issue on the minds of many people these days, one way to slow it down is to adopt a plant-based diet. People who are following this type of lifestyle, leave less carbon footprint. The water and land consumption due to farming are also decreased, which overall benefits the entire planet.

How Do You Start A Plant-Based Diet?

From eating bacon in the morning to stews and steaks at dinners, most of us center our eating habits around the meat. To start a plant-based diet, one should mainly focus on fruits and vegetables and other plant-based products rather than processed foods and meats. The quality of the food should be given more thought and reducing animal-based product quantity.

- Focus mainly on Vegetables

Replace your main dishes from meat to vegetable-based. Half of your plate should at least be filled with colorful vegetables. Try making salads, salsa, and other side dishes to go with your mains.

- Use less amount of red meat

Try to reduce the meat from your eating pattern as much as possible. At first, use it as a side or a garnish than slowly cut it down.

- Eat good fats

Fats are important nutrients needed for healthy functioning. There are many plant sources where you can get fats like avocado, nuts and olive oil, etc. They have a good type of fat that keeps your LDL low and keeps your heart healthy.

- Eat whole grains

They are rich in fiber and cut down on appetite quick. In the morning, eating a bowl of oatmeal or barley is a good choice. Adding different varieties of nuts can also be helpful.

- Eat more fruits

People get a craving for sugar when they suddenly stop eating it for a few days. To control that desire, fruits can be looked at as an alternative to calm down the sweet tooth.

- Prefer more green leafy vegetables

Green leafy vegetables have a good number of vitamins and fiber. There is also a great variety to choose from, such as kale, spinach, Swiss chard, etc. They will help you remain full throughout the day.

What to Eat

You can eat:

Grains – all whole-grains and lentils are allowed including millets, quinoa, brown rice, amaranth, quinoa, all beans, whole-grain flour, coconut flour, almond flour, and baked products like bread, bagels, and pasta

Nuts – all nuts are allowed

Seeds – all seeds are allowed

Vegetables – all organically grown vegetables are allowed, including onion, tomatoes, bell pepper, cauliflower, broccoli, sprouts, asparagus, radish, collard, kale, spinach, chards, etc.

Fruits – all organically fruits are allowed, including banana, apple, pineapple, grapes, oranges, all berries, avocado, watermelon, etc.

Meat – Use plant-based alternates to meat such as tempeh, seitan, and tofu

Milk – plant-based alternate for milk like almond milk, coconut milk, hazelnut milk, soymilk, etc.

Dairy – plant-based alternate for dairies like peanut butter, almond butter, cashew butter, almond yogurt, cashew yogurt, plant-based cheeses, etc.

Egg – replace regular eggs with flax eggs

Sugar – coconut sugar, maple syrup, honey, stevia, Splenda, etc.

Drink – unsweetened juices and smoothies, unsweetened tea and coffee made with plant-based milk, etc.

What to Avoid

You cannot eat:

Meat – All meat and their by-products are not allowed like beef, pork, and poultry, lamb, goat, chicken, sausage, hot dogs, etc.

Seafood – all fishes and seafood are not allowed

Dairy – dairy items are not allowed like eggs, whole milk, yogurt, etc.

Drink – sweetened drinks are not allowed, such as sweetened fruit juices, soda, sweetened tea, and coffee, etc.

Other – fried food, fast foods

White bread

White pasta

Tips for Staying Committed to Plant-Based Diet

It might be difficult to follow this diet in the beginning, but with the benefits it has to offer, it is worthwhile to. The body does not accept sudden changes and will try to make you go back to your old routine. You need to constantly push down the desires and keep strong in times of weakness. All people feel some amount of craving and hunger, but their will to self-restraint is far stronger. There are many ways to keep yourself on the right track of eating healthy, which includes:

- Know when you crave and be prepared

Some people like salty snacks and others, sweets. It's up to you how to replace these carvings. Switching to fruits whenever you feel like eating chocolates or candy and eating crunchy vegetables or whole-grain crackers whenever bored can help you to be more in control. Bring salted nuts to the movies instead of buying popcorn.

- Have someone look over you

We can easily cheat our diets if no one is keeping us accountable. Making your partner or a friend hold you accountable can help you stay on track of your goals and not get distracted. You are more likely to follow a diet if the person close to you is making sure that you are following it correctly.

- Make Vegetarian meals

Even if you are not going full vegan and leaving meat is hard, at least make one meal a week that is fully comprised of vegetables. Plan out the ingredients and recipes over the weekend so that when the time comes, you will be ready to make your dish.

- Make your meals fun

It is easy to lose interest after a couple of days, but to stay motivated; you have to be innovative. Try out new vegetables that you have never eaten before or look up new recipes. Try to make your blend of dishes with a healthy list of ingredients.

Chapter 2: Air Fryer 101

What Is an Air Fryer?

With great technology coming through the market day after day, one device has changed the way we see deep-fried foods. An Air Fryer is a kitchen device made for multi-purpose cooking. It can be used for many different functions such as grilling, frying, roasting, and baking. People often confuse this new appliance with stove pressure cookers, but they are two very different devices. An air fryer is a smaller device than a pressure cooker. It is also way easier to clean it because of its small size. A pressure cooker is mainly used to handle liquids and soups, while an Air Fryer is not designed for liquid use. Any item that requires any form deep or pan-frying, it is better done with an air fryer.

Air Fryer has a modern design that even makes it look portable. Its compact design also helps in cooking food quickly. It comprises a timer which is used to set the time of cooking of each food. It also has a temperature controller like an oven so that you have more control over the cooking process. Different types of food require different times and temperatures. It has a stainless-steel frying basket to put food in. It is recommended to keep checking the food every 20 minutes; the time will continue even if the frying basket is taken out. The temperature ranges from 175F to 400F.

Advantages of Using an Air Fryer

The Air Fryer is becoming more and more popular these days; everyone is talking about how to make your meals more oil-free and healthier. This device achieves so much that it is very difficult not to discuss it these days. Many of its advantages include:

- Diversity

It has a diverse set of uses from grilling, roasting frying, and so much more. It cuts down the need for buying more appliances because of its vast range of uses. It can cook many different types of foods as well from chips, chicken wings, or burgers. All of the items need a different time of cooking, but all are cooked efficiently with this device.

- Oil-free

People that are calorie conscious or just looking for a way to reduce fat in their diet, Air Fryer is the device they can use. Its way of cooking by circulating heated air around the cooking basket with almost no use of oil makes the dishes healthier and lighter in consumption.

- Reheating food

When reheating leftovers or cold delivery food, you want to preserve the taste and freshness as much as you can. The air fryer does the job perfectly.

- Time management

Everyone spends so much on fast food because it is convenient and saves them a lot of time. This often comes with the cost of one's health. With an air fryer, quick recipes can be made with ease without the usual compromise on health.

- Reduce Kitchen injuries

With no use of oil, a lot of injuries come down too. You might have been burnt by the sizzle of a hot oil many times, but this risk reduces to nil with the use of air fryer.

How Does It Work?

As new devices are produced, our daily lives have become more and more easy. Air Fryer has made use of modern technology to help us navigate the kitchen effortlessly.

An Air Fryer is a very user-friendly device that works like a miniature convection oven. It has a power turbo countertop convection oven, which is its main unit. It cooks food by using a convection mechanism where hot air is circulated inside the machine cooking the food inside with crispiness and evenness. Convection is a process of transferring heat between particles. Hot air because it is denser, goes down the machine, and the cooler air rises.

Its method of cooking is better than other convection ovens and is also faster because of its small size. The small size speeds up the process of convection significantly. It has an electric coil that is inside the lid and a fan situated on top of the machine. When it is turned on, the electric coil in the machine heats, to desired set temperature, the compact air around it. The fan rotates that hot air through the entire compartment. The frying basket containing the food receives the hot air constantly throughout the time that it has been set to. This makes the food cook evenly with its taste all intact. The intensity of heat gives it its crispiness with no use of oil at all.

How to Start Cooking in An Air Fryer?

Air Fryer is very easy to use the device, and even someone with no experience can operate it without a glitch.

1. Place the Air Fryer over a heat resistant surface such as a marble counter and make sure that it has some space behind for the air to flow out. Make sure to place it where it cannot be damaged.
2. Now open the lid and remove the frying basket, it can be greased by oil if required by a brush.
3. As Air Fryer is like a miniature oven, it also needs to be preheated before use.
4. Load the frying basket with the food that needs to be cooked. Do not fill the entire basket but leave a third of its portion empty so air can circulate.
5. Put the frying basket inside the machine, secure it tightly, and shut the lid.
6. Put the power port inside a socket and turn on the electricity, the indicators of time and temperature will light up, showing that it is turned on. Set the time and temperature based on what type of food you are preparing.
7. Constantly check the food every 15 to 20 min by shaking, stirring, or flipping the contents.
8. When the cooking process is finished, a beep will be heard, and the device will shut down automatically. Give it a minute to shut down fully.
9. Take out the food from the frying basket and serve it hot on a plate.
10. Set the fryer aside, and don't use it until the device cools down. Clean the device before using it again.

How to Clean and Maintain Your Air Fryer

It is recommended to clean the Air Fryer every month thoroughly. If you fail to do so, then the machine will start to accumulate filth and give off an unpleasant smell. Also, during the cooking process, it might release black smoke from behind. This is no cause for alarm, but it might affect the overall taste of your food. Unlike cooking like the old days, the Air Fryer only has a frying basket utensil that will need cleaning rather than an array of spoons and pans. The frying basket can become greasy over time with multiple uses, so its cleaning is vital. Here are the steps on how to clean your device

1. First, switch off the device, then put the electric cord neatly down, and wait till the device completely cools down.

2. Now, take off the lid and take out the frying basket. It might be greasy, and food particles may be stuck on the bottom. To remove them, put a lot of water in a large container and mix in dishwater soap. Leave the frying basket in the solution for 10 to 15 minutes.

3. Do not use abrasive cleaning techniques and equipment that can remove the stainless-steel coating of the basket.

4. Later, take it out and scrub it down with a sponge.

5. Pat the basket gently, dry it using a kitchen towel or a napkin. After it is perfectly dry, reinsert it into the machine.

Chapter 3: 21-Day Meal plan

Day	Breakfast	Lunch	Dinner	Dessert
1	Broccoli	Rainbow Vegetables Salad	Pineapple and Tofu Kabobs	Stuffed and Spiced Baked Apples
2	Breakfast Potatoes	Plantain Chips	Vegetable Salad with Chimichurri Vinaigrette	Stuffed and Spiced Baked Apples
3	Breakfast Potatoes	Cauliflower and Broccoli Bites	Roasted Vegetable and Pasta Salad	Brownies
4	Omelets	Mushroom Pizzas	Roasted Vegetable and Pasta Salad	Brownies
5	Omelets	Roasted Butternut Squash Salad	Cauliflower Stir-Fry	Apple and Blueberries Crumble
6	French Toast	Black Bean Burger	Parmesan Eggplant with Pasta	Mug Carrot Cake
7	French Toast	Kale Chips	Parmesan Eggplant with Pasta	Donut Holes
8	Tofu and Potato Scramble	Fried Chickpea Salad	Thai Style Crab Cakes	Donut Holes
9	Tofu and Potato Scramble	Sweet Potato Croutons Salad	Thai Style Crab Cakes	Cinnamon Churros
10	Eggplant Bacon	Tofu Buddha Bowl	Fish Taco Wraps	Cinnamon Churros
11	Falafel	Sweet Potatoes and Brussels sprouts Bowls	Fish Taco Wraps	Peanut Butter Balls
12	Breakfast Sandwich	Italian Tofu Salad	Jackfruit Taquitos	Peanut Butter Balls
13	Breakfast Sandwich	Avocado Fries	Tofu and Cauliflower Rice	Baked Apples
14	Loaded Hash Browns	Green Bean and Mushroom Casserole	Tofu and Cauliflower Rice	Baked Apples

15	Loaded Hash Browns	Green Bean and Mushroom Casserole	Tempeh Kabobs	Sweet Potato Dessert Fries
16	Balsamic Tofu Bacon	Maple Roasted Brussels sprouts	Cauliflower and Chickpea Tacos	Sweet Potato Dessert Fries
17	Broccoli	Baby Bok Choy	Cauliflower and Chickpea Tacos	Donuts
18	Breakfast Potatoes	Popcorn Tofu	Roasted Butternut Squash with Mushrooms and Cranberries	Donuts
19	French Toast	Spicy Sweet Potato Fries	Buffalo Cauliflower Wing	Stuffed and Spiced Baked Apples
20	French Toast	Corn and Zucchini Fritters	Buffalo Cauliflower Wing	Brownies
21	Tofu and Potato Scramble	Fried Ravioli	Cheesy Potatoes	Brownies

Chapter 4: Breakfast and Brunch

French Toast

Preparation time: 5 minutes
Cooking time: 12 minutes
Servings: 4

Ingredients:

- 4 slices of bread, whole-grain
- ½ cup rolled oats
- ½ cup pecans
- 1 tablespoon ground flax seed
- ½ teaspoon ground cinnamon
- 1/3 cup almond milk
- Maple syrup for serving
- Olive oil spray

Method:

1. Switch on the air fryer, insert the fryer basket, then shut it with the lid, set the frying temperature 350 degrees F, and let it preheat for 5 minutes.
2. Meanwhile, prepare the topping and for this, place oats in a food processor, add flax seeds, pecans, and cinnamon it and pulse for 2 minutes until the mixture resembles breadcrumbs.
3. Tip the mixture in a shallow dish, take another shallow dish, and pour milk in it.
4. Add bread slices, one at a time, and then let them soak for 15 seconds until side, don't let it mushy.
5. Open the preheated fryer, place prepared bread slices in it in a single layer, spray with olive oil, close the lid and cook for 6 minutes until golden brown and cooked, turning and spraying with oil halfway.
6. When done, the air fryer will beep, then open the lid, transfer the toast to a dish, sprinkle the prepared topping on it, and cover with foil to keep it warm.
7. Prepare the remaining toast in the same manner, sprinkle with remaining topping, and serve straight away.

Nutrition Value:

- Calories: 102.2 Cal
- Fat: 3.4 g
- Carbs: 28.2 g

- Protein: 6.2 g
- Fiber: 3.6 g

Loaded Hash Browns

Preparation time: 25 minutes
Cooking time: 20 minutes
Servings: 4

Ingredients:

- 3 medium russet potatoes, peeled, grated
- 1/4 cup chopped red peppers
- 1/4 cup chopped white onions
- 1/4 cup chopped green peppers
- 1 teaspoon minced garlic
- ½ teaspoon ground black pepper
- 1 teaspoon paprika
- 2/3 teaspoon salt
- 2 teaspoons olive oil

Method:

1. Take a medium bowl, place grated potatoes in it, cover with chilled water, and let it soak for 20 minutes.
2. Then drain the potatoes, pat dry with paper towels, place them in a bowl and add all the spices and oil until stir until combined.
3. Switch on the air fryer, insert the baking basket, add potatoes, then shut it with the lid, set the frying temperature 400 degrees F, and cook for 10 minutes until golden brown and cooked, shaking halfway.
4. Then add onions and peppers, shake until mixed, shut the fryer with lid and continue cooking for 10 minutes until cooked.
5. When done, the air fryer will beep and then open the lid and transfer potatoes to a dish.
6. Serve straight away.

Nutrition Value:

- Calories: 200 Cal
- Fat: 6.5 g
- Carbs: 7 g
- Protein: 3.5 g
- Fiber: 1 g

Tofu and Potato Scramble

Preparation time: 10 minutes
Cooking time: 30 minutes
Servings: 3

Ingredients:

- 1 block of tofu, pressed, drained, cut into 1-inch pieces
- 4 cups broccoli florets
- 1/2 cup chopped white onion
- 4 medium potatoes, peeled, 1-inch cubed
- 1/2 teaspoon onion powder
- 1/2 teaspoon garlic powder
- 1 teaspoon turmeric
- 2 tablespoons soy sauce
- 2 tablespoons olive oil, divided

Method:

1. Take a medium bowl, add tofu pieces in it, add onion, sprinkle with onion powder, garlic powder, and turmeric, drizzle with 1 tablespoon oil and soy sauce, toss until coated, and let it marinate for 15 minutes.
2. Meanwhile, switch on the air fryer, insert the fryer basket, then shut it with the lid, set the frying temperature 400 degrees F, and let it preheat for 5 minutes.
3. In the meantime, place potatoes in a small bowl, drizzle with remaining oil and toss until well coated.
4. Open the preheated fryer, place potatoes in it, close the lid and cook for 15 minutes until golden brown and cooked, shaking halfway.
5. Then add tofu into the fryer, reserving the marinade, shut with lid, and continue cooking for 10 minutes at 370 degrees F until cooked, shaking halfway.
6. Meanwhile, add broccoli florets into the reserved marinade and toss until well coated.
7. When 10 minutes of frying time is up, add broccoli florets into the fryer, toss until mixed, shut with lid, and continue cooking for 5 minutes until cooked, shaking halfway.

8. When done, the air fryer will beep and then open the lid and transfer scramble to a dish.
9. Serve straight away.

Nutrition Value:

- Calories: 286 Cal
- Fat: 20.7 g
- Carbs: 10.3 g

- Protein: 19.4 g
- Fiber: 3.3 g

Breakfast Sandwich

Preparation time: 10 minutes
Cooking time: 10 minutes
Servings: 4

Ingredients:

For the Tofu:

- 1 block of tofu, pressed, drained, cut into four round slices
- 1 teaspoon garlic powder
- 1/8 teaspoon paprika
- 1/2 teaspoon ground turmeric
- 1/4 cup soy sauce
- Olive oil spray

For the Sandwich:

- 1 medium avocado, peeled, pitted, sliced
- 4 slices of white onion
- 4 slices of tomato
- 4 tablespoons vegan mayonnaise
- 4 slices of vegan cheese
- 4 English muffins, whole-grain

Method:

1. Take a shallow dish, place tofu slices in it, add remaining ingredients for the tofu in it, toss until well coated, then cover the dish and let it marinate for a minimum of 10 minutes.
2. Meanwhile, switch on the air fryer, insert the fryer basket, then shut it with the lid, set the frying temperature 400 degrees F, and let it preheat for 10 minutes.
3. Then open the preheated fryer, place tofu in it in a single layer, spray with olive oil, close the lid and cook for 10 minutes until golden brown and cooked, turning and spraying with oil halfway.
4. When done, the air fryer will beep and then open the lid and transfer tofu to a plate.

5. Prepare the sandwich and for this, cut each muffin into half, then spread 1 tablespoon of mayonnaise in the bottom of each muffin and top with a slice of avocado, cheese, onion, and tomato.

6. Place a tofu slice on the topping, cover with the top half of the muffin and serve straight away.

Nutrition Value:

- Calories: 380 Cal
- Fat: 14 g
- Carbs: 45 g

- Protein: 21 g
- Fiber: 17 g

Omelets

Preparation time: 10 minutes
Cooking time: 21 minutes
Servings: 4

Ingredients:

- ½ block of tofu, pressed, drained
- ¼ cup chickpea flour
- 3 tablespoons chopped kale
- 3 tablespoons chopped spinach
- 3 tablespoons chopped dried mushrooms
- ¼ teaspoon garlic powder
- ¼ teaspoon onion powder
- ¼ teaspoon ground black pepper
- ¼ teaspoon salt
- ½ teaspoon turmeric powder
- ¼ teaspoon dried basil
- ½ teaspoon cumin powder
- 3 tablespoons nutritional yeast
- 1 tablespoon Braggs
- ½ cup grated vegan cheese
- 1 tablespoon water
- Olive oil spray

Method:

1. Take a food processor, place all the ingredients in it except for cheese and vegetables and pulse for 2 minutes until batter comes together.
2. Transfer the batter into a large bowl, add cheese and chopped vegetables and mix until combined.
3. Switch on the air fryer, insert the fryer basket, then shut it with the lid, set the frying temperature 370 degrees F, and let it preheat for 5 minutes.
4. Meanwhile, prepare the omelet and for this, place a piece of parchment paper on working space, place a desired shape cookie cutter on it, press one-sixth of the prepared batter in it, and then lift the cookie cutter.

5. Prepare five more omelets in the same manner on the parchment sheet.
6. Open the preheated fryer, place omelets in it in a single layer, spray with olive oil, close the lid and cook for 8 minutes until golden brown and cooked, turning and spraying with oil halfway.
7. When done, the air fryer will beep and then open the lid, transfer omelets to a dish and cover with a foil to keep them warm.
8. Cook remaining omelets in the same manner and then serve straight away.

Nutrition Value:

- Calories: 104.6 Cal
- Fat: 1.9 g
- Carbs: 10.2 g
- Protein: 11.3 g
- Fiber: 0.3 g

Balsamic Tofu Bacon

Preparation time: 35 minutes
Cooking time: 40 minutes
Servings: 4

Ingredients:

- 1 block of tofu, pressed, drained, sliced
- 1 teaspoon garlic powder
- 1/4 cup soy sauce
- 1 tablespoon maple syrup
- 1 tablespoon liquid smoke
- 3 tablespoons balsamic vinegar
- Olive oil spray

Method:

1. Prepare the marinade and for this, take a small bowl, add garlic powder and then stir in soy sauce, maple syrup, liquid smoke, and vinegar until combined.
2. Cut tofu into slices, place them in a shallow dish, pour in prepared marinade, toss until well coated, and then marinate in the refrigerator for 30 minutes.
3. When ready to cook, switch on the air fryer, insert the fryer basket, then shut it with the lid, set the frying temperature 400 degrees F, and let it preheat for 5 minutes.
4. Then open the preheated fryer, place tofu slices in it in a single layer, spray with olive oil, close the lid and cook for 20 minutes until golden brown and cooked, turning and spraying with oil halfway.
5. When done, the air fryer will beep and then open the lid, transfer tofu slices to a dish and cover with a foil to keep them warm.
6. Cook remaining tofu slices in the same manner and then serve straight away.

Nutrition Value:

- Calories: 372.9 Cal
- Fat: 27.7 g
- Carbs: 33.6 g
- Protein: 26 g
- Fiber: 4 g

Falafel

Preparation time: 50 minutes
Cooking time: 35 minutes
Servings: 12

Ingredients:

- 15-ounce cooked chickpeas
- 3/4 cup minced white onion
- 2 teaspoons minced garlic
- 1/3 cup chopped parsley
- 1/4 teaspoon ground black pepper
- 1/4 teaspoon sea salt
- 2 tablespoons sesame seeds
- 1/8 teaspoon ground cardamom
- 1/8 teaspoon ground coriander
- 1 1/2 teaspoon cumin
- 4 tablespoons almond flour
- Panko bread crumbs as needed for coating
- Olive oil spray

Method:

1. Take a food processor, place chickpeas in it, add the next nine ingredients, pulse for 2 minutes until a crumbly dough comes together, and then blend in flour, 1 tablespoon at a time until the dough comes together.
2. Transfer the dough to a large bowl, cover with a plastic wrap and freeze for 45 minutes until firm.
3. Then switch on the air fryer, insert the fryer basket, then shut it with the lid, set the frying temperature 375 degrees F, and let it preheat for 5 minutes.
4. Meanwhile, shape the falafel mixture into twelve patties and then dredge into bread crumbs.
5. Open the preheated fryer, place falafel in it in a single layer, spray with olive oil, close the lid and cook for 15 minutes until golden brown and cooked, turning and spraying with oil halfway.

6. When done, the air fryer will beep, then open the lid, transfer falafel to a dish and cover with foil to keep them warm.
7. Cook the remaining falafel in the same manner and then serve straight away.

Nutrition Value:

- Calories: 91 Cal
- Fat: 5.8 g
- Carbs: 8.1 g
- Protein: 2.2 g
- Fiber: 1.6 g

Eggplant Bacon

Preparation time: 10 minutes
Cooking time: 30 minutes
Servings: 4

Ingredients:

- 1 medium eggplant, destemmed
- 1 teaspoon lemon juice
- 1/2 teaspoon ground black pepper
- 1/2 teaspoon salt
- 1 teaspoon smoked paprika
- 1/2 teaspoon cumin
- 1 teaspoon maple syrup
- 2 tablespoons soy sauce
- 1/4 teaspoon Worcestershire sauce, vegan
- 1 tablespoon toasted sesame oil
- 1 tablespoon olive oil
- Olive oil spray

Method:

1. Switch on the air fryer, insert the fryer basket, then shut it with the lid, set the frying temperature 300 degrees F, and let it preheat for 5 minutes.
2. Meanwhile, prepare the eggplant and for this, cut it into quarters, and then slice it into 1/8-thick long strips like bacon.
3. Take a small bowl, add remaining ingredients in it, stir until combined, and then brush the mixture on both sides of eggplant strips.
4. Open the preheated fryer, place eggplant strips in it in a single layer, spray with olive oil, close the lid and cook for 15 minutes until golden brown and dried, turning and spraying with oil halfway.
5. When done, the air fryer will beep, then open the lid, transfer eggplant strips to a dish and cover with foil to keep them warm.
6. Cook remaining eggplant strips in the same manner and then serve straight away.

Nutrition Value:

- Calories: 99 Cal
- Fat: 7.2 g
- Carbs: 8.9 g

- Protein: 1.7 g
- Fiber: 4.3 g

Breakfast Potatoes

Preparation time: 35 minutes
Cooking time: 30 minutes
Servings: 4

Ingredients:

- 3 large potatoes, peeled, ½-inch cubed
- 1 small red pepper, diced
- 1 teaspoon onion powder
- 1 medium white onion, peeled, diced
- 1 teaspoon garlic powder
- 1 teaspoon paprika
- 2 teaspoons sea salt
- 2 tablespoons olive oil

Method:

1. Place potatoes in a large bowl, cover them with chilled water and let them soak for 30 minutes.
2. Meanwhile, take a small bowl, place all the seasonings in it and stir until mixed, set aside until required.
3. Switch on the air fryer, insert the fryer basket, then shut it with the lid, set the frying temperature 370 degrees F, and let it preheat for 5 minutes.
4. Then drain the soaked potatoes, pat dries them, place them in a large bowl, drizzle with oil and mix until coated.
5. Open the preheated fryer, place potatoes in it, close the lid and cook for 20 minutes until golden brown and cooked, shaking halfway.
6. When done, the air fryer will beep and then open the lid and transfer potatoes to a large bowl.
7. Add diced onion and red pepper, mix well and then stir in prepared seasoning mix until coated.
8. Transfer the potato mixture into the fryer basket, spray with olive oil, close the lid and cook for 10 minutes at 380 degrees F until cooked, shaking halfway.
9. Serve straight away.

Nutrition Value:

- Calories: 135 Cal
- Fat: 2 g
- Carbs: 27 g

- Protein: 4 g
- Fiber: 3 g

Broccoli

Preparation time: 5 minutes
Cooking time: 15 minutes
Servings: 2

Ingredients:

- 4 cups broccoli florets
- 2/3 teaspoon ground black pepper
- 1 ½ teaspoon salt
- 1 tablespoon nutritional yeast
- 2 tablespoons olive oil

Method:

1. Switch on the air fryer, insert the fryer basket, then shut it with the lid, set the frying temperature 370 degrees F, and let it preheat for 5 minutes.
2. Meanwhile, take a large bowl, place florets in it, add remaining ingredients and toss until well mixed.
3. Open the preheated fryer, place florets in it in a single layer, close the lid and cook for 5 minutes until golden brown and cooked, shaking, and spraying with oil halfway.
4. When done, the air fryer will beep, then open the lid, transfer broccoli to a dish and cover with foil to keep it warm.
5. Cook remaining broccoli florets in the same manner and then serve straight away.

Nutrition Value:

- Calories: 176 Cal
- Fat: 14 g
- Carbs: 7 g
- Protein: 3 g
- Fiber: 4 g

Chapter 5: Appetizer and Snacks

Spiced Chickpeas

Preparation time: 5 minutes
Cooking time: 20 minutes
Servings: 4

Ingredients:

- 19 ounces cooked chickpeas
- 3/4 teaspoon salt
- 2 teaspoons tandoori spice blend
- 1 tablespoon olive oil

Method:

1. Switch on the air fryer, insert the fryer basket, then shut it with the lid, set the frying temperature 390 degrees F, and let it preheat for 5 minutes.
2. Meanwhile, take a large bowl, place chickpeas in it, add remaining ingredients and toss until mixed.
3. Open the preheated fryer, place half of the chickpeas in it, close the lid and cook for 10 minutes until golden brown and cooked, shaking halfway.
4. When done, the air fryer will beep, then open the lid, transfer chickpeas to a dish and cover with foil to keep them warm.
5. Cook the remaining half of the chickpeas in the same manner and serve straight away.

Nutrition Value:

- Calories: 140 Cal
- Fat: 5 g
- Carbs: 17 g
- Protein: 6 g
- Fiber: 4 g

Fried Ravioli

Preparation time: 5 minutes
Cooking time: 24 minutes
Servings: 4

Ingredients:

- 8 ounces frozen vegan ravioli, thawed
- 1 teaspoon garlic powder
- 1 teaspoon dried oregano
- ¼ teaspoon ground black pepper
- ¼ teaspoon salt
- 1 teaspoon dried basil
- 2 teaspoons nutritional yeast
- 1/2 cup panko bread crumbs
- 1/4 cup chickpeas liquid
- 1/2 cup marinara
- Olive oil spray

Method:

1. Switch on the air fryer, insert the fryer basket, then shut it with the lid, set the frying temperature 390 degrees F, and let it preheat for 5 minutes.
2. Meanwhile, place bread crumbs in a shallow dish, add nutritional yeast and all the herbs and spices and stir until mixed.
3. Take a bowl, pour in chickpeas liquid in it, then dip ravioli in it and dredge into bread crumbs mixture until evenly coated.
4. Open the preheated fryer, place ravioli in it in a single layer, spray with olive oil, close the lid and cook for 12 minutes until golden brown and cooked, turning and spraying with oil halfway.
5. When done, the air fryer will beep, then open the lid, transfer ravioli to a dish and cover with foil to keep them warm.
6. Cook remaining ravioli in the same manner and then serve straight away.

Nutrition Value:

- Calories: 150 Cal
- Fat: 2 g
- Carbs: 27 g
- Protein: 5 g
- Fiber: 2 g

Sweet Potato Tots

Preparation time: 5 minutes
Cooking time: 28 minutes
Servings: 25

Ingredients:

- 2 cups sweet potato puree
- 1/2 teaspoon ground cumin
- 1/2 teaspoon salt
- 1/2 teaspoon ground coriander
- 1/2 cup Panko breadcrumbs
- Olive oil spray

Method:

1. Switch on the air fryer, insert the fryer basket, then shut it with the lid, set the frying temperature 390 degrees F, and let it preheat for 5 minutes.
2. Meanwhile, take a large bowl, place all the ingredients in it, stir until well combined, and then shape the mixture into twenty-five tots, each about 1 tablespoon.
3. Open the preheated fryer, place sweet potato tots in it in a single layer, spray with olive oil, close the lid and cook for 14 minutes until golden brown and cooked, turning and spraying with oil halfway.
4. When done, the air fryer will beep, then open the lid, transfer tots to a dish and cover with foil to keep them warm.
5. Cook remaining tots in the same manner and then serve straight away.

Nutrition Value:

- Calories: 26 Cal
- Fat: 0.2 g
- Carbs: 6 g
- Protein: 0 g
- Fiber: 2 g

Kale Chips

Preparation time: 5 minutes
Cooking time: 5 minutes
Servings: 2

Ingredients:

- 4 cups kale leaves, stems removed
- 1/4 teaspoon salt
- 2 teaspoons ranch seasoning, vegan
- 1 tablespoon nutritional yeast
- 2 tablespoons olive oil

Method:

1. Switch on the air fryer, insert the fryer basket, then shut it with the lid, set the frying temperature 370 degrees F, and let it preheat for 5 minutes.
2. Meanwhile, take a medium bowl, add kale chips and remaining ingredients and toss until coated.
3. Open the preheated fryer, place kale in it, close the lid and cook for 5 minutes until golden brown and cooked, shaking halfway.
4. When done, the air fryer will beep and then open the lid and transfer kale chips to a dish.
5. Serve straight away.

Nutrition Value:

- Calories: 98 Cal
- Fat: 4 g
- Carbs: 15.7 g
- Protein: 0 g
- Fiber: 2.7 g

Avocado Fries

Preparation time: 5 minutes
Cooking time: 10 minutes
Servings: 4

Ingredients:

- 1 medium avocado, peeled, pitted, sliced
- 1/2 teaspoon salt
- 1/2 cup panko breadcrumbs
- ¼ cup chickpeas liquid
- Olive oil spray

Method:

1. Switch on the air fryer, insert the fryer basket, then shut it with the lid, set the frying temperature 390 degrees F, and let it preheat for 5 minutes.
2. Meanwhile, take a shallow bowl, place breadcrumbs in it, season with salt, and stir until combined.
3. Take another shallow bowl, pour in chickpeas liquid, dip avocado slices in it and then dredge into breadcrumbs mixture until coated.
4. Open the preheated fryer, place avocado slices in it in a single layer, spray with olive oil, close the lid and cook for 10 minutes until golden brown and cooked, shaking, and spraying with oil halfway.
5. When done, the air fryer will beep and then open the lid and transfer avocado fries to a dish.
6. Serve straight away.

Nutrition Value:

- Calories: 132 Cal
- Fat: 11.1 g
- Carbs: 6.6 g
- Protein: 4 g
- Fiber: 4 g

Buffalo Cauliflower Wings

Preparation time: 10 minutes
Cooking time: 40 minutes
Servings: 4

Ingredients:

- 1 large head cauliflower, cut into florets
- 1 teaspoon minced garlic
- 1/2 cup Frank red hot sauce
- 2 tablespoons almond butter
- 1 cup of soy milk
- Olive oil spray

For the Batter:

- 1 cup almond flour
- 1/4 teaspoon dried chipotle chili
- 1/4 teaspoon cayenne pepper
- 1 teaspoon granules of chicken bouillon, vegan
- 1/4 teaspoon paprika
- 1/4 teaspoon red chili powder

Method:

1. Switch on the air fryer, insert the fryer basket, then shut it with the lid, set the frying temperature 390 degrees F, and let it preheat for 5 minutes.
2. Meanwhile, prepare the batter and for this, take a large bowl, place all its ingredients in it and whisk until smooth batter comes together.
3. Then add cauliflower florets in it and toss until well coated.
4. Open the preheated fryer, place cauliflower florets in it in a single layer, close the lid and cook for 20 minutes until golden brown and cooked, turning and spraying with oil halfway.
5. Meanwhile, prepare the sauce and for this, take a small saucepan, place it over medium-high heat, add butter in it, stir in garlic and hot sauce, bring the mixture to boil and then simmer over medium heat until thickened, covering the pan.

6. When done, the air fryer will beep, then open the lid, transfer cauliflower florets to a large dish and cover with foil to keep them warm.
7. Cook remaining cauliflower florets, in the same manner, add them to the bowl, then pour prepared sauce over them and toss until well coated.
8. Serve straight away.

Nutrition Value:

- Calories: 129 Cal
- Fat: 1 g
- Carbs: 24 g
- Protein: 7 g
- Fiber: 4 g

Baked Potatoes

Preparation time: 5 minutes
Cooking time: 40 minutes
Servings: 4

Ingredients:

- 4 large baking potatoes
- 4 tablespoons chopped parsley
- 1 teaspoon garlic powder
- 2 teaspoons ground black pepper
- 2 teaspoons salt
- 2 tablespoons olive oil
- 4 tablespoons almond butter, divided

Method:

1. Switch on the air fryer, insert the fryer basket, then shut it with the lid, set the frying temperature 400 degrees F, and let it preheat for 5 minutes.
2. Meanwhile, brush potatoes with oil, then season with garlic powder, salt, and black pepper, and sprinkle with parsley.
3. Open the preheated fryer, place potatoes in it, close the lid and cook for 40 minutes until golden brown and cooked, turning and spraying with oil halfway.
4. When done, the air fryer will beep and then open the lid and transfer potatoes to a dish.
5. Open the potatoes by slicing them in half lengthwise, top each potato with 1 tablespoon of butter and serve.

Nutrition Value:

- Calories: 161 Cal
- Fat: 0.2 g
- Carbs: 37 g
- Protein: 4.3 g
- Fiber: 3.8 g

Roasted Almonds

Preparation time: 5 minutes
Cooking time: 6 minutes
Servings: 8

Ingredients:

- 2 cups almonds
- 1 tablespoon garlic powder
- 1/4 teaspoon ground black pepper
- 1 teaspoon paprika
- 1 tablespoon soy sauce

Method:

1. Switch on the air fryer, insert the fryer basket, then shut it with the lid, set the frying temperature 320 degrees F, and let it preheat for 5 minutes.
2. Meanwhile, take a large bowl, add almonds in it, then add remaining ingredients and toss until mixed.
3. Open the preheated fryer, place almonds in it, close the lid and cook for 6 minutes until golden brown and cooked, shaking halfway.
4. When done, the air fryer will beep and then open the lid and transfer almonds to a dish.
5. Serve straight away.

Nutrition Value:

- Calories: 7.7 Cal
- Fat: 0.7 g
- Carbs: 0.3 g
- Protein: 0.3 g
- Fiber: 0.1 g

Zucchini Chips

Preparation time: 5 minutes
Cooking time: 24 minutes
Servings: 4

Ingredients:

- 1/2 cup almond flour
- 1 large zucchini, ¼-inch thick sliced
- 1/2 teaspoon garlic powder
- 1 teaspoon onion powder
- 1/2 teaspoon salt
- 1 teaspoon Italian seasoning
- 1/4 cup nutritional yeast
- 1/4 cup almond milk, unsweetened
- Olive oil spray

Method:

1. Switch on the air fryer, insert the fryer basket, then shut it with the lid, set the frying temperature 390 degrees F, and let it preheat for 5 minutes.
2. Meanwhile, place zucchini slices in a bowl, drizzle with milk and toss until coated.
3. Then take a shallow dish, place flour in it along with remaining ingredients, stir until combined, and then dredge each zucchini slice in it until evenly coated.
4. Open the preheated fryer, place zucchini slices in it in a single layer, spray with olive oil, close the lid and cook for 12 minutes until golden brown and cooked, turning and spraying with oil halfway.
5. When done, the air fryer will beep, then open the lid, transfer zucchini chips to a dish and cover with foil to keep them warm.
6. Cook remaining zucchini chips in the same manner and serve.

Nutrition Value:

- Calories: 165 Cal
- Fat: 1.2 g
- Carbs: 6 g
- Protein: 1.6 g
- Fiber: 2.2 g

Croutons

Preparation time: 5 minutes
Cooking time: 10 minutes
Servings: 4

Ingredients:

- 2 cups cubed bread, whole-grain
- 1/2 teaspoon garlic powder
- 1/3 teaspoon salt
- 1/2 teaspoon dried basil
- 1/4 teaspoon ground black pepper
- 1/2 teaspoon dried oregano
- 2 teaspoons lemon juice
- 2 teaspoons olive oil

Method:

1. Switch on the air fryer, insert the fryer basket, then shut it with the lid, set the frying temperature 400 degrees F, and let it preheat for 5 minutes.
2. Meanwhile, take a large bowl, place bread cubes in it, drizzle with lemon juice and oil, then sprinkle with remaining ingredients and toss until coated.
3. Open the preheated fryer, place croutons in it in a single layer, spray with olive oil, close the lid and cook for 5 minutes until golden brown and cooked, turning and spraying with oil halfway.
4. When done, the air fryer will beep, then open the lid, transfer croutons to a dish and cover with foil to keep them warm.
5. Cook remaining croutons in the same manner and serve.

Nutrition Value:

- Calories: 30 Cal
- Fat: 1 g
- Carbs: 4 g
- Protein: 0 g
- Fiber: 1 g

Chapter 6: Main Dishes

Pineapple and Tofu Kabobs

Preparation time: 15 minutes
Cooking time: 30 minutes
Servings: 4

Ingredients:

- 1 medium pineapple, cubed
- 1 block of tofu, firmed, pressed, drained
- 1 medium white onion, peeled, cut into large chunks
- 2 medium green bell peppers, cored, cut into large chunks
- Soaked wooden skewers

For the Marinade:

- 1/2 teaspoon ground ginger
- 1/2 teaspoon paprika
- 1/2 cup tamari
- 1/4 cup maple syrup
- 1/2 cup water

Method:

1. Prepare the marinade and for this, take a shallow dish, place all its ingredients in it and whisk until combined.
2. Cut tofu into cubes, then add them into the marinade, toss until coated, and let them stand for 10 minutes.
3. Then Switch on the air fryer, insert the fryer basket, then shut it with the lid, set the frying temperature 320 degrees F, and let it preheat for 5 minutes.
4. Meanwhile, prepare kabobs, and for this, thread tofu alternating with the vegetables in the skewers.
5. Open the preheated fryer, place prepared kabobs in it in a single layer, spray with olive oil, close the lid and cook for 15 minutes until golden brown on all sides and cooked through, shaking and spraying with oil halfway.

6. When done, the air fryer will beep, then open the lid, transfer kabobs to a dish and cover with foil to keep them warm.
7. Cook remaining kabobs in the same manner and serve straight away.

Nutrition Value:

- Calories: 630 Cal
- Fat: 21 g
- Carbs: 83 g
- Protein: 31 g
- Fiber: 5 g

Cauliflower and Broccoli Bites

Preparation time: 5 minutes
Cooking time: 12 minutes
Servings: 4

Ingredients:

- 1 cup panko bread crumbs
- ¼ cup grated vegan parmesan cheese
- 1 tablespoon creole seasoning
- 2 cups cauliflower florets
- 2 cups broccoli florets
- ½ cup whole-wheat flour
- 2 flax eggs
- 1 tablespoon chopped parsley
- Marinara sauce as needed for serving

Method:

1. Switch on the air fryer, insert the fryer basket, spray it with olive oil, then shut it with the lid, set the frying temperature 400 degrees F, and let it preheat for 5 minutes.
2. Meanwhile, take a large bowl, add bread crumbs in it and stir in seasoning and cheese until mixed, set aside until required.
3. Place flax eggs in another bowl, and then place flour in a shallow dish.
4. Prepare florets and for this, dredge broccoli and cauliflower florets into the flour, then dip into the flax eggs and coat with bread crumbs mixture until coated.
5. Open the preheated fryer, place florets in it in a single layer, spray with olive oil, close the lid and cook for 6 minutes until golden brown and cooked, shaking, and spraying with oil halfway.
6. When done, the air fryer will beep, then open the lid, transfer florets to a dish, and cover with a foil to keep them warm.
7. Cook remaining florets, in the same manner, sprinkle with parsley and serve with marinara sauce.

Nutrition Value:

- Calories: 130 Cal
- Fat: 3.5 g
- Carbs: 20 g
- Protein: 8 g
- Fiber: 2 g

Cauliflower Stir-Fry

Preparation time: 5 minutes
Cooking time: 30 minutes
Servings: 4

Ingredients:

- 3/4 cup of onion white, peeled, sliced
- 1 large head of cauliflower, cut into florets
- 2 teaspoons minced garlic
- 1/2 teaspoon coconut sugar
- 1 tablespoon rice vinegar
- 1 1/2 tablespoons tamari
- 1 tablespoon Sriracha sauce
- 2 scallions, chopped
- Olive oil spray

Method:

1. Switch on the air fryer, insert the fryer baking pan, then shut it with the lid, set the frying temperature 350 degrees F, and let it preheat for 5 minutes.
2. Then add cauliflower florets, spray with olive oil, close the lid and cook for 10 minutes until golden brown, shaking halfway.
3. When done, the air fryer will beep, open the lid, add onion, stir until mixed, continue cooking for 10 minutes, then add garlic, stir until mixed, cook for 5 minutes.
4. Meanwhile, prepare the sauce and for this, place remaining ingredients in a small bowl and whisk until combined.
5. When vegetables have cooked, pour prepared sauce over them, toss until coated, and cook for another 5 minutes.
6. When done, transfer vegetables to a dish, sprinkle with scallions, and serve.

Nutrition Value:

- Calories: 93 Cal
- Fat: 3 g
- Carbs: 12 g
- Protein: 4 g
- Fiber: 3 g

Parmesan Eggplant with Pasta

Preparation time: 5 minutes
Cooking time: 16 minutes
Servings: 4

Ingredients:

- 1/2 cup almond flour
- 1 large eggplant, destemmed, sliced
- 1/3 teaspoon garlic powder
- 1/3 teaspoon onion powder
- ¼ teaspoon ground black pepper
- 1/3 teaspoon salt
- 1/2 cup panko bread crumbs
- 1/2 cup almond milk, unsweetened
- 2 tablespoons vegan grated parmesan

For the Topping:

- 1/2 cup shredded vegan mozzarella cheese
- 1 cup marinara sauce and more as needed for serving
- 1/3 cup grated vegan parmesan cheese

For Serving:

- 12 ounces cooked whole-grain pasta
- 1/3 cup vegan grated parmesan cheese
- 3 tablespoons chopped parsley

Method:

1. Switch on the air fryer, insert the fryer basket, then shut it with the lid, set the frying temperature 400 degrees F, and let it preheat for 5 minutes.
2. Meanwhile, place bread crumbs in a shallow dish and stir in garlic powder, onion powder, black pepper, salt, and cheese until mixed.
3. Take another shallow dish, place flour in it, then take a bowl and pour milk in it.
4. Prepare eggplants and for this, coat each slice with flour, then dip into milk and dredge with bread crumbs mixture until coated on both sides.

5. Open the preheated fryer, place eggplant slices in it in a single layer, spray with olive oil, close the lid and cook for 15 minutes until golden brown and cooked, turning and spraying with oil halfway.
6. When done, the air fryer will beep, then open the lid, top with marinara sauce and both cheeses, shut with lid, and cook for 1 minute until cheese has melted.
7. When done, transfer eggplant slices to a dish, add cooked pasta, garnish with parsley and parmesan cheese and serve.

Nutrition Value:

- Calories: 449.9 Cal
- Fat: 10.3 g
- Carbs: 41.7 g
- Protein: 22.5 g
- Fiber: 12 g

Mushroom Pizzas

Preparation time: 10 minutes
Cooking time: 6 minutes
Servings: 4

Ingredients:

- 4 kalamata olives, sliced
- 2 tablespoons diced sweet red pepper
- 4 large caps of Portobello mushrooms, destemmed
- 3 ounces shredded zucchini
- 2 tablespoons minced basil
- ½ teaspoon minced garlic
- 1 teaspoon ground black pepper
- 2 teaspoons salt
- 1 teaspoon dried basil
- 2 tablespoons balsamic vinegar
- 4 tablespoons pasta sauce
- 1/2 cups hummus
- Olive oil spray

Method:

1. Switch on the air fryer, insert the fryer basket, then shut it with the lid, set the frying temperature 330 degrees F, and let it preheat for 5 minutes.
2. Meanwhile, prepare the mushroom caps, remove the stem and gills, and brush with vinegar.
3. Season mushrooms with half of each salt and black pepper, then spread 1 tablespoon of pasta sauce into each mushroom and sprinkle with garlic.
4. Open the preheated fryer, place mushrooms in it in a single layer, close the lid and cook for 3 minutes.
5. When done, the air fryer will beep, open the lid, take out the mushrooms and top evenly with red pepper, olives, and zucchini, sprinkle with dried basil and remaining black pepper and salt.
6. Return stuffed mushrooms into the baking basket, shut with lid, and continue cooking for 3 minutes until mushrooms are fork-tender.

7. When done, transfer mushrooms to a dish, drizzle with mined basil and hummus and serve.
8. Serve straight away.

Nutrition Value:

- Calories: 70 Cal
- Fat: 1.6 g
- Carbs: 11 g
- Protein: 4.3 g
- Fiber: 3.5 g

Thai Style Crab Cakes

Preparation time: 15 minutes
Cooking time: 40 minutes
Servings: 8

Ingredients:

- ¾ cup artichoke hearts, chopped
- 4 cups cubed potatoes
- 7 ounces hearts of palm, grated
- 1 bunch green onions, diced
- 1½-inch piece of ginger
- 2/3 teaspoon ground black pepper
- 1 teaspoon salt
- 1 lime, zested, juiced
- 4 tablespoons Thai Red Curry Paste
- 1 tablespoon soy sauce
- 4 sheets of nori
- Olive oil spray

Method:

1. Place potato cubes to a medium pot, cover them with water, place it over medium-high heat and boil for 5 to 8 minutes until fork tender.
2. Meanwhile, cut nori sheet into pieces, add them into a food processor along with onion and ginger, then add curry paste, soy sauce, lime juice, and zest and pulse for 2 minutes until the smooth paste comes together, set aside until required.
3. When potatoes have boiled, drain them, cool them for 10 minutes, then place them in a large bowl, add the prepared paste and stir well until combined.
4. Add artichokes and hearts of palm, stir until mixed, and then shape the mixture into eight patties.
5. Switch on the air fryer, insert the fryer basket, then shut it with the lid, set the frying temperature 350 degrees F, and let it preheat for 5 minutes.
6. Open the preheated fryer, place patties in it in a single layer, spray with olive oil, close the lid and cook for 15 minutes until golden brown and cooked, turning and spraying with oil halfway.

7. When done, the air fryer will beep, then open the lid, transfer patties to a dish and cover with foil to keep them warm.
8. Cook remaining patties in the same manner and serve straight away.

Nutrition Value:

- Calories: 97 Cal
- Fat: 0.4 g
- Carbs: 20 g
- Protein: 4 g
- Fiber: 5 g

Black Bean Burger

Preparation time: 20 minutes
Cooking time: 15 minutes
Servings: 6

Ingredients:

- 1 1/3 cups rolled oats
- 1/2 cup corn kernels
- 12 ounces cooked black beans
- 1/2 teaspoon garlic powder
- 1 1/4 teaspoons red chili powder
- 1 tablespoon soy sauce
- 1/2 teaspoon chipotle chili powder
- 3/4 cup tomato salsa
- Olive oil spray

Method:

1. Switch on the air fryer, insert the fryer basket, then shut it with the lid, set the frying temperature 375 degrees F, and let it preheat for 5 minutes.
2. Meanwhile, take a food processor, add oats in it and pulse for five-time until oats are partially chipped.
3. Then remaining ingredients in it, except for corn, pulse for 1 minute until blended, and tip the mixture in a bowl.
4. Stir in corn, cover the bowl with a plastic wrap, place in the refrigerator for 15 minutes until chilled, and then shape the mixture into six burgers.
5. Open the preheated fryer, place bean burgers in it in a single layer, spray with olive oil, close the lid and cook for 15 minutes until golden brown and cooked, turning and spraying with oil halfway.
6. When done, the air fryer will beep and then open the lid and transfer black bean burgers to a dish.
7. Serve straight away.

Nutrition Value:

- Calories: 158 Cal
- Fat: 1.3 g
- Carbs: 30 g
- Protein: 8 g
- Fiber: 9 g

Tofu Buddha Bowl

Preparation time: 10 minutes
Cooking time: 25 minutes
Servings: 6

Ingredients:

- 8 ounces spinach, sautéed with garlic in olive oil
- 2 cups cooked quinoa
- 3 medium carrots, peeled, sliced
- 14 ounces tofu, extra-firm, cut into small cubes
- 1 pound broccoli florets
- 1 medium red bell pepper, cored, sliced
- 3 tablespoons molasses
- 1/4 cup soy sauce
- 1 tablespoon Sriracha sauce
- 2 tablespoons lime juice
- 2 tablespoons sesame oil
- Olive oil spray

Method:

1. Prepare the marinade and for this, take a large bowl, add lime juice in it, whisk in molasses, Sriracha sauce, soy sauce, and sesame oil until combined, add tofu pieces in it, toss until well coated and marinate for 10 minutes, stirring occasionally.
2. Then switch on the air fryer, insert the fryer basket, spray with oil, then shut it with the lid, set the frying temperature 370 degrees F, and let it preheat for 5 minutes.
3. Open the preheated fryer, place tofu in it, close the lid and cook for 15 minutes until golden brown and cooked, shaking every 5 minutes.
4. Meanwhile, place all the vegetables into the marinade, except for spinach, toss until mixed and set aside until required.
5. When done, the air fryer will beep, open the lid, transfer tofu to a dish, add marinated vegetables in the fryer basket, shut with lid, and cook for 10 minutes, shaking halfway.

6. When done, assemble the bowl and for this, place quinoa in a large bowl, top with vegetables, spinach, and tofu in the ends, sprinkle with sesame seeds, drizzle with remaining marinade and serve.

Nutrition Value:

- Calories: 236 Cal
- Fat: 8 g
- Carbs: 31 g
- Protein: 12 g
- Fiber: 6 g

Sweet Potatoes and Brussels sprouts Bowls

Preparation time: 10 minutes
Cooking time: 25 minutes
Servings: 4

Ingredients:

- 2 cups cooked quinoa
- 1/3 cup Tahini Dressing
- 1/3 cup peanut butter sauce
- 1/4 cup chopped green onion

For the Veggies:

- 4 cups sliced Brussels sprouts
- 6 cups diced sweet potato
- 2 teaspoons garlic powder, divided
- 2 tablespoons soy sauce

Method:

1. Switch on the air fryer, insert the fryer basket, then shut it with the lid, set the frying temperature 400 degrees F, and let it preheat for 5 minutes.
2. Then open the preheated fryer, place sweet potatoes in it, spray with olive oil, sprinkle with 1 teaspoon of garlic powder, shake well, close the lid and cook for 15 minutes until golden brown, shaking halfway.
3. When done, the air fryer will beep, open the lid, add sprouts, spray with oil, and sprinkle with remaining garlic powder, shake well to mix, close the lid and cook for 5 minutes until tender.
4. When done, drizzle soy sauce over vegetables, shake until mixed, shut with lid and continue cooking for 5 minutes until cooked and browned, shaking halfway.
5. Assemble the bowls and for this, divide quinoa between four bowls, top with vegetables, drizzle with peanut butter sauce and tahini dressing and sprinkle with green onion.
6. Serve straight away.

Nutrition Value:

- Calories: 357 Cal
- Fat: 26.1 g
- Carbs: 28.4 g

- Protein: 8.9 g
- Fiber: 6.3 g

Fish Taco Wraps

Preparation time: 5 minutes
Cooking time: 12 minutes
Servings: 4

Ingredients:

- 2 cobs of grilled corns
- 1 small white onion, peeled, diced
- 4 pieces of Fishless Filet
- 1 small red bell pepper, cored, deseeded, diced
- 4 large tortillas, burrito-size
- ½ cup Mango Salsa
- Mixed green as needed
- Tortilla chips as needed
- 4 tablespoons shredded vegan parmesan cheese
- Olive oil spray

Method:

1. Switch on the air fryer, insert the fryer basket, then shut it with the lid, set the frying temperature 400 degrees F, and let it preheat for 5 minutes.
2. Then open the preheated fryer, place fillets in it in a single layer, spray with olive oil, close the lid and cook for 6 minutes until golden brown and cooked, turning and spraying with oil halfway.
3. Meanwhile, take a skillet pan, place it over medium heat, grease it with oil and when hot, add onion and bell pepper and cook for 5 minutes until softened.
4. Then stir in corn until mixed, continue cooking for 2 minutes until hot, and set aside until required.
5. When done, the air fryer will beep, then open the lid and transfer fillets to a dish.
6. Assemble tacos and for this, evenly spoon one-fourth of the cooked onion-pepper mixture into a tortilla, top with a fish fillet, 2 tablespoons of mango salsa, tortilla chips, mixed greens and grated cheese in the end.
7. Place prepared tacos into the fryer basket, shut with lid, and cook at 350 degrees F for 6 minutes until cooked.
8. Serve straight away.

Nutrition Value:

- Calories: 407 Cal
- Fat: 6.4 g
- Carbs: 74.4 g
- Protein: 19.7 g
- Fiber: 24.7 g

Jackfruit Taquitos

Preparation time: 10 minutes
Cooking time: 11 minutes
Servings: 4

Ingredients:

- 4 whole-wheat tortillas, 6-inch
- 1 cup cooked red beans
- 14 ounces of jackfruit, packed in water, drained
- ¼ cup and 2 tablespoons water
- ½ cup pico de gallo
- Olive oil spray

Method:

1. Switch on the instant pot, place jackfruit and beans in the inner pot, stir in pico de gallo sauce, pour in water, and shut with lid.
2. Then press the manual button and cook for 3 minutes at a low-pressure setting and, when done, release pressure naturally.
3. Open the lid, mash the jackfruit mixture, and set aside until required.
4. Switch on the air fryer, insert the fryer basket, then shut it with the lid, set the frying temperature 370 degrees F, and let it preheat for 5 minutes.
5. Meanwhile, prepare tortillas and for this, place ¼ cup of the bean-jackfruit mixture onto each tortilla and roll it up tightly, and prepare remaining tortillas in the same manner.
6. Open the preheated fryer, place tortillas in it in a single layer, spray with olive oil, close the lid and cook for 8 minutes until golden brown and cooked.
7. When done, the air fryer will beep and then open the lid and transfer tortillas to a dish.
8. Serve straight away.

Nutrition Value:

- Calories: 230 Cal
- Fat: 7.3 g
- Carbs: 38 g
- Protein: 4.6 g
- Fiber: 3 g

Tofu and Cauliflower Rice

Preparation time: 5 minutes
Cooking time: 22 minutes
Servings: 4

Ingredients:

For the Tofu:

- 1/2 block of tofu, extra-firm, pressed, drained
- 1 cup diced carrot
- 1/2 cup diced white onion
- 2 tablespoons soy sauce
- 1 teaspoon turmeric powder

For the Cauliflower Rice:

- 1/2 cup chopped broccoli
- 3 cups riced cauliflower
- 1 tablespoon minced ginger
- 1 teaspoon minced garlic
- 1/2 cup frozen peas
- 1 tablespoon apple cider vinegar
- 2 tablespoons soy sauce
- 1 1/2 teaspoons sesame oil
- Olive oil spray

Method:

1. Switch on the air fryer, insert the fryer baking pan, then shut it with the lid, set the frying temperature 370 degrees F, and let it preheat for 5 minutes.
2. Open the preheated fryer, add all the ingredients for the tofu in it, shake well until mixed, spray with olive oil, close the lid and cook for 10 minutes, shaking halfway.
3. Meanwhile, take a large bowl, place all the ingredients for cauliflower rice in it, and stir until combined.
4. When done, the air fryer will beep, open the lid, add cauliflower rice mixture, shake well to mix, and continue cooking for 12 minutes until cooked.

5. Serve straight away.

Nutrition Value:

- Calories: 86.9 Cal
- Fat: 0.6 g
- Carbs: 16.8 g

- Protein: 4.6 g
- Fiber: 5 g

Green Bean and Mushroom Casserole

Preparation time: 5 minutes
Cooking time: 12 minutes
Servings: 6

Ingredients:

- 24 ounces green beans, trimmed
- 1/3 cup fried French onions
- 2 cups sliced button mushrooms
- 1 teaspoon onion powder
- 1 tablespoon garlic powder
- 3/4 teaspoon ground black pepper
- 3/4 teaspoon salt
- 3/4 teaspoon ground sage
- 1 lemon, juiced
- Olive oil spray

Method:

1. Switch on the air fryer, insert the fryer basket, then shut it with the lid, set the frying temperature 400 degrees F, and let it preheat for 5 minutes.
2. Meanwhile, take a large bowl, place all the ingredients in it, except for French onions, and stir until mixed.
3. Open the preheated fryer, place green beans mixture in it, spray with olive oil, close the lid and cook for 12 minutes until golden brown and cooked, shaking halfway.
4. When done, the air fryer will beep and then open the lid and transfer green beans to a dish.
5. Garnish green beans with fried onions and serve straight away.

Nutrition Value:

- Calories: 83 Cal
- Fat: 3 g
- Carbs: 12.3 g
- Protein: 2.9 g
- Fiber: 3.4 g

Tempeh Kabobs

Preparation time: 2 hours and 5 minutes
Cooking time: 20 minutes
Servings: 4

Ingredients:

- 8 ounces tempeh, steamed
- 1 cup sliced button mushrooms
- 1 medium red onion, peeled, quartered
- 1 cup cherry tomato halves
- 1 small green bell pepper, cored, sliced
- Olive oil spray
- Soaked wooden skewers

For the Marinade:

- 1 ½ teaspoons minced garlic
- 1/2 teaspoon ground black pepper
- 2 teaspoons ground cumin
- 1 teaspoon maple syrup
- 1 teaspoon ground turmeric
- 2 lemons, juiced
- 1/4 cup soy sauce
- 2 teaspoons olive oil
- 3/4 cup vegetable broth

Method:

1. Prepare the marinade, and for this, take a bowl, place all of its ingredients in it and whisk until combined.
2. Cut steamed tempeh into twelve cubes, place them in a large container, add vegetables, then pour in half of the prepared marinade, toss until coated, cover the container with a lid and marinate in the refrigerator for 2 hours.
3. Then switch on the air fryer, insert the fryer basket, then shut it with the lid, set the frying temperature 390 degrees F, and let it preheat for 5 minutes.

4. Meanwhile, remove tempeh cubes and vegetables from the marinade, thread tempeh alternating with vegetables onto skewers, reserving the marinade.

5. Open the preheated fryer, place skewers in it in a single layer, spray with olive oil, close the lid, cook for 5 minutes, then brush with the marinade, turn them and continue cooking for another 5 minutes until thoroughly cooked.

6. When done, the air fryer will beep, open the lid, transfer kabobs to a dish, and cover with foil to keep them warm.

7. Cook remaining kabobs in the same manner and serve.

Nutrition Value:

- Calories: 173.2 Cal
- Fat: 2.8 g
- Carbs: 36.5 g
- Protein: 5 g
- Fiber: 7.7 g

Cauliflower and Chickpea Tacos

Preparation time: 10 minutes
Cooking time: 20 minutes
Servings: 4

Ingredients:

- 19 ounces cooked chickpeas
- 4 cups cauliflower florets, chopped
- 2 tablespoons taco seasoning
- 2 tablespoons olive oil

For Serving:

- 2 medium avocados, peeled, pitted, sliced
- Coconut yogurt as needed for drizzle
- 4 cups shredded cabbage
- 8 small tortillas

Method:

1. Switch on the air fryer, insert the fryer basket, then shut it with the lid, set the frying temperature 390 degrees F, and let it preheat for 5 minutes.
2. Meanwhile, take a large bowl, add cauliflower florets and chickpeas, sprinkle with taco seasoning, drizzle with oil and toss until combined.
3. Open the preheated fryer, place cauliflower-chickpeas in it in a single layer, close the lid and cook for 20 minutes until golden brown and cooked, shaking oil halfway.
4. When done, the air fryer will beep, then open the lid and transfer cauliflower-chickpeas mixture to a dish.
5. Distribute transfer cauliflower-chickpeas mixture evenly between tortillas, top with cabbage and avocado, drizzle with yogurt, and serve.

Nutrition Value:

- Calories: 190 Cal
- Fat: 16 g
- Carbs: 11 g
- Protein: 3 g
- Fiber: 3 g

Chapter 7: Vegetables and Sides

Roasted Corn

Preparation time: 5 minutes
Cooking time: 10 minutes
Servings: 4

Ingredients:

- 4 ears of corn, husk removed
- ½ teaspoon ground black pepper
- 1 teaspoon salt
- 3 teaspoons olive oil

Method:

1. Switch on the air fryer, insert the fryer basket, then shut it with the lid, set the frying temperature 400 degrees F, and let it preheat for 5 minutes.
2. Meanwhile, remove husk and silk from corn, rinse them well, and pat dry.
3. Then cut the corns to fit into the fryer basket, drizzle with oil and season with black pepper and salt.
4. Open the preheated fryer, place corns in it, close the lid and cook for 10 minutes until golden brown and cooked, turning halfway.
5. When done, the air fryer will beep and then open the lid and transfer corn to a dish.
6. Serve straight away.

Nutrition Value:

- Calories: 175 Cal
- Fat: 7.7 g
- Carbs: 27 g
- Protein: 4.8 g
- Fiber: 3 g

Plantain Chips

Preparation time: 5 minutes
Cooking time: 20 minutes
Servings: 2

Ingredients:

- 3 green plantains, peeled, sliced
- 1 lime, zested
- ½ teaspoon garlic powder
- 1 teaspoon of sea salt
- 1/8 teaspoon red chili powder
- 2 teaspoons olive oil
- 1 cup guacamole, for serving

Method:

1. Switch on the air fryer, insert the fryer basket, then shut it with the lid, set the frying temperature 374 degrees F, and let it preheat for 5 minutes.
2. Meanwhile, take a large bowl, add plantain slices in it along with remaining ingredients, except for guacamole and toss until coated.
3. Open the preheated fryer, place plantain in it, close the lid and cook for 20 minutes until golden brown and cooked, shaking every 5 minutes.
4. When done, the air fryer will beep and then open the lid and transfer plantain chips to a dish.
5. Serve plantain chips with guacamole.

Nutrition Value:

- Calories: 220 Cal
- Fat: 12 g
- Carbs: 25 g
- Protein: 1 g
- Fiber: 2 g

Roasted Garlic

Preparation time: 10 minutes
Cooking time: 25 minutes
Servings: 4

Ingredients:

- 1 medium head of garlic
- Olive oil spray

Method:

1. Switch on the air fryer, insert the fryer basket, then shut it with the lid, set the frying temperature 400 degrees F, and let it preheat for 5 minutes.
2. Meanwhile, remove excess peel from the garlic head, and then expose the top of garlic by removing ¼-inch off the top.
3. Spray the garlic head with oil generously and then wrap with a foil.
4. Open the preheated fryer, place wrapped garlic head in it, close the lid and cook for 25 minutes until done.
5. When done, the air fryer will beep, then open the lid, transfer garlic to a dish and let it cool for 5 minutes.
6. Then squeeze the garlic out of its skin and serve with warmed garlic or as desired.

Nutrition Value:

- Calories: 160 Cal
- Fat: 2.5 g
- Carbs: 27 g
- Protein: 6 g
- Fiber: 3 g

Maple Roasted Brussels sprouts

Preparation time: 5 minutes
Cooking time: 10 minutes
Servings: 2

Ingredients:

- 2 cups Brussels sprouts, ¼-inch thick sliced
- 1/4 teaspoon sea salt
- 1 tablespoon balsamic vinegar
- 1 tablespoon maple syrup

Method:

1. Switch on the air fryer, insert the fryer basket, then shut it with the lid, set the frying temperature 400 degrees F, and let it preheat for 5 minutes.
2. Meanwhile, take a large bowl, add Brussel sprouts in it, season with salt, drizzle with vinegar and maple syrup and toss until well coated.
3. Open the preheated fryer, place Brussel sprouts in it, close the lid and cook for 10 minutes until golden brown and cooked, shaking halfway.
4. When done, the air fryer will beep, then open the lid and transfer Brussel sprouts to a dish.
5. Serve straight away.

Nutrition Value:

- Calories: 85.3 Cal
- Fat: 3.3 g
- Carbs: 13.1 g
- Protein: 2.8 g
- Fiber: 2.8 g

Roasted Butternut Squash with Mushrooms and Cranberries

Preparation time: 5 minutes
Cooking time: 30 minutes
Servings: 6

Ingredients:

- 4 cups diced butternut squash
- 1 cup sliced green onions
- 8 ounces button mushrooms, destemmed, quartered
- ¼ cup dried cranberries

For the Sauce:

- 1 tablespoon maple syrup
- 4 cloves of garlic, peeled
- 1 tablespoon soy sauce
- 1 tablespoon balsamic vinegar
- 1 tablespoon olive oil

Method:

1. Switch on the air fryer, insert the fryer basket, then shut it with the lid, set the frying temperature 400 degrees F, and let it preheat for 5 minutes.
2. Meanwhile, prepare the sauce and for this, place all of its ingredients in a food processor and puree for 1 minute until blended.
3. Take a large bowl, place all the vegetables and berries, add sauce and toss until coated.
4. Open the preheated fryer, place vegetables in it, close the lid and cook for 30 minutes until golden brown and cooked, shaking every 10 minutes.
5. When done, the air fryer will beep, then open the lid, transfer vegetables and berries to a dish and garnish with some more green onions.
6. Serve straight away.

Nutrition Value:

- Calories: 128 Cal
- Fat: 2.6 g
- Carbs: 28 g
- Protein: 2.2 g
- Fiber: 8.6 g

Roasted Green Beans

Preparation time: 5 minutes
Cooking time: 10 minutes
Servings: 2

Ingredients:

- 8 ounces green beans, trimmed
- 1 teaspoon sesame oil
- 1 tablespoon soy sauce

Method:

1. Switch on the air fryer, insert the fryer basket, then shut it with the lid, set the frying temperature 400 degrees F, and let it preheat for 5 minutes.
2. Meanwhile, snap the green beans into half, place them in a large bowl, add oil and soy sauce and toss until well coated.
3. Open the preheated fryer, place green beans in it, spray with olive oil, close the lid and cook for 10 minutes until golden brown and cooked, shaking halfway.
4. When done, the air fryer will beep and then open the lid and transfer green beans to a dish.
5. Serve straight away.

Nutrition Value:

- Calories: 33.2 Cal
- Fat: 2.5 g
- Carbs: 2.7 g
- Protein: 0.7 g
- Fiber: 1.3 g

Shishito Peppers

Preparation time: 5 minutes
Cooking time: 6 minutes
Servings: 4

Ingredients:

- 20 Shishito peppers
- 1 teaspoon salt
- Olive oil spray

Method:

1. Switch on the air fryer, insert the fryer basket, then shut it with the lid, set the frying temperature 390 degrees F, and let it preheat for 5 minutes.
2. Open the preheated fryer, place peppers in it, spray well with olive oil, close the lid and cook for 6 minutes until cooked and lightly charred, shaking halfway.
3. When done, the air fryer will beep, open the lid, transfer peppers to a dish, and season with salt.
4. Serve straight away.

Nutrition Value:

- Calories: 21 Cal
- Fat: 1 g
- Carbs: 5 g
- Protein: 1 g
- Fiber: 2 g

Baby Bok Choy

Preparation time: 5 minutes
Cooking time: 6 minutes
Servings: 4

Ingredients:

- 4 bunches of babies bok choy
- 1 teaspoon garlic powder
- Olive oil spray

Method:

1. Switch on the air fryer, insert the fryer basket, then shut it with the lid, set the frying temperature 350 degrees F, and let it preheat for 5 minutes.
2. Meanwhile, prepare the bok choy and for this, slice off the bottom, separate the leaves, rinse and drain well.
3. Open the preheated fryer, place bok choy in it, spray generously with olive oil, sprinkle with garlic powder, shake well, close the lid and cook for 6 minutes until golden brown and cooked, shaking halfway.
4. When done, the air fryer will beep, then open the lid and transfer bok choy to a dish.
5. Serve straight away.

Nutrition Value:

- Calories: 58 Cal
- Fat: 2 g
- Carbs: 5 g
- Protein: 1 g
- Fiber: 1 g

Popcorn Tofu

Preparation time: 5 minutes
Cooking time: 24 minutes
Servings: 4

Ingredients:

- 14 ounces tofu, extra-firm, pressed, drained
- 1 ½ cup panko bread crumbs

For the Batter:

- 1 teaspoon onion powder
- 1/2 cup cornmeal
- 1/2 cup chickpea flour
- 1 teaspoon garlic powder
- 1/2 teaspoon ground black pepper
- 1/2 teaspoon salt
- 1 tablespoon Vegetarian Bouillon
- 2 tablespoons nutritional yeast
- 1 tablespoon Dijon mustard
- 3/4 cup almond milk, unsweetened

Method:

1. Switch on the air fryer, insert the fryer basket, then shut it with the lid, set the frying temperature 350 degrees F, and let it preheat for 5 minutes.
2. Meanwhile, prepare the batter and for this, place all of its ingredients in a large bowl and then whisk until combined until smooth batter comes together.
3. Take a shallow dish and then place bread crumbs in it.
4. Cut tofu into bite-size pieces, dip into prepared batter and then dredge with bread crumbs until coated on both sides.
5. Open the preheated fryer, place tofu in it in a single layer, spray with olive oil, close the lid and cook for 12 minutes until golden brown and cooked, shaking halfway.
6. When done, the air fryer will beep, open the lid, transfer popcorns to a dish, and cover with foil to keep them warm.
7. Cook remaining tofu popcorns in the same manner and then serve.

Nutrition Value:

- Calories: 261 Cal
- Fat: 5.5 g
- Carbs: 37.5 g

- Protein: 16 g
- Fiber: 4.8 g

Spicy Sweet Potato Fries

Preparation time: 5 minutes
Cooking time: 25 minutes
Servings: 6

Ingredients:

- 2 large sweet potatoes, peeled
- 2 teaspoons olive oil

For the Seasoning Mix:

- 2 teaspoons salt
- 1 teaspoon ground fennel
- 2 teaspoons ground coriander
- 1 teaspoon Aleppo pepper
- 1 teaspoon dried oregano

Method:

1. Switch on the air fryer, insert the fryer basket, then shut it with the lid, set the frying temperature 350 degrees F, and let it preheat for 5 minutes.
2. Meanwhile, prepare the fries and for this, cut sweet potatoes into ½-inch fries, place them in a large bowl, and then drizzle with oil.
3. Prepare the seasoning mix, and for this, place all of its ingredients in a blender and pulse until ground.
4. Sprinkle the ground seasoning over sweet potatoes and then toss until well coated.
5. Open the preheated fryer, place sweet potatoes fries in it, close the lid and cook for 25 minutes until golden brown and cooked, shaking halfway.
6. When done, the air fryer will beep and then open the lid and transfer chips to a dish.
7. Serve straight away.

Nutrition Value:

- Calories: 34.4 Cal
- Fat: 0.1 g
- Carbs: 7.9 g
- Protein: 0.5 g
- Fiber: 1 g

Cheesy Potatoes

Preparation time: 5 minutes
Cooking time: 18 minutes
Servings: 4

Ingredients:

For the Potatoes:

- 1 pound fingerling potatoes, washed, halved
- 1 teaspoon ground black pepper
- 1/2 teaspoon garlic powder
- 1 teaspoon salt
- 1 teaspoon olive oil

For the Cheese Sauce:

- 2 tablespoons nutritional yeast
- 1/2 teaspoon paprika
- 1/2 teaspoon ground turmeric
- 1/2 cup cashews
- 1 teaspoon lemon juice
- 1/4 cup water

Method:

1. Switch on the air fryer, insert the fryer basket, then shut it with the lid, set the frying temperature 400 degrees F, and let it preheat for 5 minutes.
2. Meanwhile, prepare the potatoes and for this, cut each potato into half, place them in a large bowl, all remaining ingredients in it, and toss until coated.
3. Open the preheated fryer, place potatoes in it, close the lid and cook for 16 minutes until golden brown and cooked, shaking halfway.
4. Meanwhile, prepare the cheese sauce and, for this, place all of its ingredients in a food processor, except for water, and blend on low until combined.
5. Then slowly blend in water until sauce reaches to desired consistency and set it aside until required.
6. When done, the air fryer will beep, open the lid, transfer potato wedges to a fryer baking pan, and drizzle with cheese sauce.

7. Insert baking pan into the air fryer, shut with lid, and cook at 400 degrees F for 2 minutes.
8. Serve straight away.

Nutrition Value:

- Calories: 238 Cal
- Fat: 12.5 g
- Carbs: 25 g
- Protein: 8.5 g
- Fiber: 3.8 g

Corn and Zucchini Fritters

Preparation time: 5 minutes
Cooking time: 16 minutes
Servings: 4

Ingredients:

- 2 medium zucchini, grated, moisture squeezed out
- 1 medium potato, peeled, grated, cooked
- 2 tablespoons chickpea flour
- 1 teaspoon minced garlic
- ½ teaspoon ground black pepper
- 1 teaspoon salt
- 1 cup corn kernels
- 2 teaspoons olive oil

Method:

1. Switch on the air fryer, insert the fryer basket, then shut it with the lid, set the frying temperature 360 degrees F, and let it preheat for 5 minutes.
2. Meanwhile, take a large bowl, add all the ingredients in it, except for oil, stir until combined, then shape the mixture into small twelve patties, each about 2 tablespoons of the batter and brush them with oil on both sides.
3. Open the preheated fryer, place patties in it in a single layer, and cook for 8 minutes until golden brown and cooked, turning halfway.
4. When done, the air fryer will beep, open the lid, transfer fritters to a dish, and cover with foil to keep them warm.
5. Cook remaining patties in the same manner and serve straight away.

Nutrition Value:

- Calories: 114.1 Cal
- Fat: 6.1 g
- Carbs: 12.8 g
- Protein: 2.6 g
- Fiber: 0.9 g

Chapter 8: Salads

Rainbow Vegetables Salad

Preparation time: 5 minutes
Cooking time: 20 minutes
Servings: 4

Ingredients:

- 1 medium red bell pepper, deseeded, diced
- 1/2 of medium sweet onion, cut into wedges
- 1 medium yellow summer squash, diced
- 1 zucchini, diced
- 4 ounces mushrooms, halved
- 1/3 teaspoon ground black pepper
- 2/3 teaspoon salt
- 1 tablespoon olive oil

Method:

1. Switch on the air fryer, insert the fryer basket, then shut it with the lid, set the frying temperature 350 degrees F, and let it preheat for 5 minutes.
2. Meanwhile, take a large bowl, place all the vegetables in it, drizzle with oil, season with salt and black pepper and toss until coated.
3. Open the preheated fryer, place vegetables in it, close the lid and cook for 20 minutes until golden brown and cooked, shaking halfway.
4. When done, the air fryer will beep, open the lid and transfer vegetables to a dish.
5. Serve straight away.

Nutrition Value:

- Calories: 69 Cal
- Fat: 3.8 g
- Carbs: 7.7 g
- Protein: 2.6 g
- Fiber: 2.3 g

Vegetable Salad with Chimichurri Vinaigrette

Preparation time: 5 minutes
Cooking time: 30 minutes
Servings: 4

Ingredients:

For the Salad:

- 1/2 head of medium purple cauliflower, cut into small florets
- 2 cups baby arugula
- 3 small red beets, peeled, 1/4-inch thick diced
- 1/2 head of medium white cauliflower, cut into small florets
- 1 medium head of frisee, torn into small pieces
- 1/2 head of medium yellow cauliflower, cut into small florets
- 6 breakfast radishes, peeled, sliced
- 1 1/3 teaspoon salt
- ¾ teaspoon ground black pepper
- 1 small bunch of mint, slivered
- Olive oil spray

For the Vinaigrette:

- 1 clove of garlic, peeled
- 1/2 bunch of chives, chopped
- 1 lemon, juiced
- 1 bunch of cilantro, leaves chopped
- 1 medium shallot, peeled, chopped
- 1 bunch parsley, leaves chopped
- 1/3 teaspoon ground black pepper
- 1/8 teaspoon red pepper flakes
- 2/3 teaspoon salt
- 1/2 cup olive oil
- 1/4 cup red wine vinegar

Method:

1. Switch on the air fryer, insert the fryer basket, then shut it with the lid, set the frying temperature 360 degrees F, and let it preheat for 5 minutes.
2. Meanwhile, place white, yellow, and purple cauliflower in separate large bowls, place beets in another bowl, then season all the cauliflower and beets with salt and black pepper, drizzle with oil and toss until well coated.
3. Open the preheated fryer, place seasoned white cauliflower in it in a single layer, close the lid and cook for 8 minutes until golden brown and cooked, shaking halfway.
4. When done, the air fryer will beep, open the lid, transfer florets to a dish and then cook yellow cauliflower and purple cauliflower separately in the same manner.
5. When cauliflowers have roasted, add beets into the fryer basket in a single layer, close the lid and cook for 14 minutes until golden brown and cooked, shaking halfway.
6. Meanwhile, prepare the vinaigrette and for this, place all of its ingredients in a food processor, except for oil, pulse for 1 minute and then slowly blend in oil until smooth.
7. Assemble the salad and for this, place all the roasted vegetables in a large bowl, pour in vinaigrette, and toss until well coated.
8. Then add remaining vegetables, toss until mixed, garnish with mint and serve.

Nutrition Value:

- Calories: 434 Cal
- Fat: 19.1 g
- Carbs: 59.5 g
- Protein: 11.5 g
- Fiber: 12.5 g

Roasted Vegetable and Pasta Salad

Preparation time: 10 minutes
Cooking time: 1 hour and 35 minutes
Servings: 16

Ingredients:

- 4 cups whole-grain pasta, cooked
- 3 small eggplants, destemmed
- 2 medium green bell peppers, deseeded, chopped
- 4 medium tomatoes, cut in eighths
- 3 medium zucchini, trimmed
- 1 cup cherry tomatoes, sliced
- 2 teaspoons salt
- ½ cup Italian dressing
- 2 tablespoons olive oil
- 8 tablespoons grated parmesan cheese
- Olive oil spray

Method:

1. Switch on the air fryer, insert the fryer basket, then shut it with the lid, set the frying temperature 350 degrees F, and let it preheat for 5 minutes.
2. Meanwhile, cut the eggplant into ½-inch thick round slices, place them in a bowl, drizzle with 1 tablespoon oil and toss until coated.
3. Open the preheated fryer, place eggplant pieces in it, close the lid, and cook for 40 minutes until cooked and very tender, shaking halfway.
4. Meanwhile, cut zucchini into ½-inch thick round slices, place them in a bowl, drizzle with 1 tablespoon oil and toss until coated.
5. When done, the air fryer will beep, open the lid and transfer eggplant to a dish.
6. Place zucchini into the fryer basket, close the lid, and cook for 25 minutes until cooked and very tender, shaking halfway.
7. When done, the air fryer will beep, open the lid and transfer zucchini to a dish containing eggplant.
8. Place tomato slices into the fryer basket, spray with olive oil, close the lid and cook for 30 minutes until cooked and very tender, shaking halfway.

9. Then take a large salad bowl, place peppers in it, then add cherry tomatoes and all the roasted vegetables, add remaining ingredients and toss until well mixed.

10. Chill the salad for 20 minutes in the refrigerated and then serve straight away.

Nutrition Value:

- Calories: 121 Cal
- Fat: 4 g
- Carbs: 23 g
- Protein: 5 g
- Fiber: 4 g

Taco Salad Bowl

Preparation time: 10 minutes
Cooking time: 7 minutes
Servings: 4

Ingredients:

- 1 flour tortilla, burrito size
- Olive oil spray
- Taco filling as needed

Method:

1. Switch on the air fryer, then shut it with the lid, set the frying temperature 400 degrees F, and let it preheat for 5 minutes.
2. Meanwhile, spray tortilla with oil on both sides, then double over with a large piece of foil on both sides; it should be slightly larger than a tortilla, press it into the fryer basket and shape it into a bowl by placing ramekins in the middle.
3. Open the preheated fryer, insert the fryer basket, close the lid and cook for 5 minutes, then remove the ramekin and foil and continue cooking for 2 minutes until the edges of the tortilla are golden brown.
4. When done, the air fryer will beep, open the lid, and lift out the taco bowl.
5. Let it cool for 10 minutes, then fill it with favorite stuffing and serve.

Nutrition Value:

- Calories: 82 Cal
- Fat: 4 g
- Carbs: 9 g
- Protein: 1 g
- Fiber: 2 g

Roasted Butternut Squash Salad

Preparation time: 10 minutes
Cooking time: 15 minutes
Servings: 4

Ingredients:

- 1 small shallot, peeled, minced
- 1 small butternut squash, peeled, deseeded, 1-inch cubed
- 1 small apple, cored, sliced
- 6 ounces arugula
- 1/4 teaspoon salt
- 1/4 teaspoon cayenne pepper
- 1 teaspoon all-purpose seasoning
- 2 tablespoons lemon juice
- 4 tablespoons olive oil
- 1/2 cup toasted sliced almonds
- 1/2 cup grated vegan Parmesan cheese

Method:

1. Switch on the air fryer, insert the fryer basket, then shut it with the lid, set the frying temperature 400 degrees F, and let it preheat for 5 minutes.
2. Meanwhile, take a large bowl, place squash in it, seasoning with all-purpose seasoning and cayenne pepper, drizzle with 2 tablespoons oil and toss until coated.
3. Open the preheated fryer, place squash in it, close the lid and cook for 15 minutes until golden brown and cooked, shaking halfway.
4. Meanwhile, take a large bowl, place shallots in it, season with salt, drizzle with lemon juice and remaining olive oil, whisk until combined, add arugula and toss until coated.
5. When done, the air fryer will beep and then open the lid and transfer squash to a plate.
6. Assemble the salad and for this, distribute arugula between four plates, top with apples and roasted squash and then sprinkle with cheese and almonds.
7. Chill the salad for 15 minutes in the refrigerator and then serve straight away.

Nutrition Value:

- Calories: 249 Cal
- Fat: 13 g
- Carbs: 35 g
- Protein: 5 g
- Fiber: 6.2 g

Fried Chickpea Salad

Preparation time: 5 minutes
Cooking time: 10 minutes
Servings: 4

Ingredients:

- 1 1/2 cups cooked chickpeas
- 1/2 teaspoon onion powder
- 1/8 teaspoon salt
- 2 teaspoons nutritional yeast
- Olive oil spray

For the Salad:

- ¼ cup chopped green onion
- ¼ cup chopped tomatoes
- 2 tablespoons chopped green chilies

Method:

1. Switch on the air fryer, insert the fryer basket, then shut it with the lid, set the frying temperature 400 degrees F, and let it preheat for 5 minutes.
2. Meanwhile, take a bowl, add chickpeas in it, spray generously with oil, add onion, salt and yeast and toss until mixed.
3. Open the preheated fryer, place chickpeas in it, close the lid and cook for 7 minutes until golden brown and cooked, shaking halfway.
4. When done, the air fryer will beep, then open the lid and transfer chickpeas to a salad bowl.
5. Cool chickpeas for 10 minutes, then add all the ingredients for the salad in it and toss until mixed.
6. Serve straight away.

Nutrition Value:

- Calories: 105 Cal
- Fat: 1 g
- Carbs: 17 g
- Protein: 5 g
- Fiber: 4 g

Sweet Potato Croutons Salad

Preparation time: 5 minutes
Cooking time: 20 minutes
Servings: 4

Ingredients:

- 12s-ounce baked sweet potato, skin-on, cut into pieces
- 2 mandarin oranges, peeled, segmented, halved
- 1-pound mixed salad greens and vegetables
- 1 sweet apple, cored, diced, air fried
- 2 tablespoons balsamic vinegar
- 1/3 cup pomegranate seeds

Method:

1. Switch on the air fryer, insert the fryer basket, then shut it with the lid, set the frying temperature 350 degrees F, and let it preheat for 5 minutes.
2. Meanwhile, prepare sweet potatoes, and for this, dice them into small pieces.
3. Open the preheated fryer, place sweet potatoes in it in a single layer, spray with olive oil, close the lid and cook for 20 minutes until golden brown and cooked, shaking halfway.
4. When done, the air fryer will beep, open the lid, and then transfer sweet potato croutons to a salad bowl.
5. Add remaining ingredients, gently stir until combined, and then serve.

Nutrition Value:

- Calories: 205 Cal
- Fat: 14 g
- Carbs: 15 g
- Protein: 5 g
- Fiber: 2 g

Brussel sprouts Salad

Preparation time: 5 minutes
Cooking time: 9 minutes
Servings: 2

Ingredients:

- 12 Brussel sprouts, cored, leaves removed
- 1 ½ tablespoons capers
- 2 tablespoons toasted sliced almonds
- 2 teaspoons chopped parsley
- 1/8 teaspoon ground black pepper
- 1/8 teaspoon red chili flakes
- 1/8 teaspoon salt
- 1 ½ tablespoon red wine vinegar
- 2 teaspoons and 1 ½ tablespoon olive oil

Method:

1. Switch on the air fryer, insert the fryer basket, then shut it with the lid, set the frying temperature 400 degrees F, and let it preheat for 5 minutes.
2. Meanwhile, take a large bowl, place sprouts in it, add 1 ½ tablespoon olive oil and toss until coated.
3. Open the preheated fryer, place sprouts in it in, close the lid and cook for 9 minutes until golden brown and cooked, shaking halfway.
4. When done, the air fryer will beep, open the lid, and transfer sprouts to a dish lined with paper towels to remove excess oil.
5. Then remove the paper towels, add remaining ingredients, and toss until combined.
6. Serve straight away.

Nutrition Value:

- Calories: 228 Cal
- Fat: 20 g
- Carbs: 11 g
- Protein: 5 g
- Fiber: 5 g

Garlic and Lemon Mushroom Salad

Preparation time: 5 minutes
Cooking time: 10 minutes
Servings: 2

Ingredients:

- 8 ounces mushrooms
- 1/2 teaspoon garlic powder
- 1 tablespoon chopped parsley
- 1 teaspoon soy sauce
- ½ teaspoon salt
- 1/3 teaspoon ground black pepper
- 2 tablespoons olive oil
- 2 wedges of lemon for serving

Method:

1. Switch on the air fryer, insert the fryer basket, then shut it with the lid, set the frying temperature 380 degrees F, and let it preheat for 5 minutes.
2. Meanwhile, cut mushrooms in quarters, then place them in a bowl, add remaining ingredients, except for lemon wedges and toss until coated.
3. Open the preheated fryer, place mushrooms in it, close the lid and cook for 10 minutes until golden brown and cooked, shaking halfway.
4. When done, the air fryer will beep, open the lid, and transfer mushrooms to the salad bowls.
5. Let mushroom cool for 10 minutes and then serve straight away.

Nutrition Value:

- Calories: 110 Cal
- Fat: 3 g
- Carbs: 15 g
- Protein: 2 g
- Fiber: 2 g

Italian Tofu Salad

Preparation time: 5 minutes
Cooking time: 10 minutes
Servings: 2

Ingredients:

- 8 ounces tofu, extra-firm, pressed, drained
- 1/2 teaspoon dried oregano
- 1/4 teaspoon onion powder
- 1/2 teaspoon garlic powder
- 1/2 teaspoon dried basil
- ¼ teaspoon ground black pepper
- 1 tablespoon soy sauce
- 1 tablespoon chickpeas liquid

Method:

1. Switch on the air fryer, insert the fryer basket, then shut it with the lid, set the frying temperature 350 degrees F, and let it preheat for 5 minutes.
2. Meanwhile, paper tofu and for this, cut tofu into ten cubed, place them in a plastic bag, add remaining ingredients, seal the bag and shake well until coated.
3. Open the preheated fryer, place tofu in it in a single layer, close the lid and cook for 10 minutes until golden brown and cooked, turning halfway.
4. When done, the air fryer will beep and then open the lid and transfer tofu to a salad bowl.
5. Serve straight away.

Nutrition Value:

- Calories: 87 Cal
- Fat: 4.4 g
- Carbs: 3.4 g
- Protein: 10 g
- Fiber: 1.3 g

Chapter 9: Desserts

Brownies

Preparation time: 5 minutes
Cooking time: 20 minutes
Servings: 4

Ingredients:

The Wet Ingredients:

- 1/4 cup almond milk
- 1/4 cup chickpeas liquid
- 1/2 teaspoon vanilla extract, unsweetened

The Dry Ingredients:

- 1/2 cup whole-wheat pastry flour
- 1/2 cup coconut sugar
- 1/4 cup cocoa powder, unsweetened
- 1 tablespoon ground flax seeds
- 1/4 teaspoon salt

For the Mix-Ins:

- 2 tablespoons chopped walnuts
- 2 tablespoons pecans
- 2 tablespoons shredded coconut

Method:

1. Switch on the air fryer, insert the fryer basket, then shut it with the lid, set the frying temperature 350 degrees F, and let it preheat for 5 minutes.
2. Meanwhile, take a large bowl, add all the dry ingredients in it and stir until mixed.
3. Take another bowl, place all the wet ingredients in it, whisk until combined, then gradually mix into the dry ingredients mixture until incorporated and mix the walnuts, pecans and coconut until combined.

4. Take a 5-inch round pan, line it with parchment paper, pour in prepared batter, smooth the top with a spatula.

5. Open the preheated fryer, place the prepared pan in it, close the lid and cook for 20 minutes until firm and a toothpick come out clean from the center of the pan.

6. When done, the air fryer will beep, then open the lid, remove the pan from the fryer and cool for 15 minutes.

7. Then cut into brownies and serve.

Nutrition Value:

- Calories: 262 Cal
- Fat: 9.9 g
- Carbs: 47.9 g
- Protein: 3.2 g
- Fiber: 4.8 g

Apple and Blueberries Crumble

Preparation time: 5 minutes
Cooking time: 15 minutes
Servings: 2

Ingredients:

- 1/2 cup frozen blueberries
- 1 medium apple, peeled, diced
- 2 tablespoons coconut sugar
- 1/4 cup and 1 tablespoon brown rice flour
- 1/2 teaspoon ground cinnamon
- 2 tablespoons almond butter

Method:

1. Switch on the air fryer, insert the fryer basket, then shut it with the lid, set the frying temperature 350 degrees F, and let it preheat for 5 minutes.
2. Meanwhile, take a large ramekin, place apples and berries in it, and stir until mixed.
3. Take a small bowl, add flour and remaining ingredients in it, stir until mixed, and then spoon this mixture over fruits.
4. Open the preheated fryer, place the prepared ramekin in it in, close the lid and cook for 15 minutes until cooked and the top has turned golden brown.
5. When done, the air fryer will beep, then open the lid and remove ramekin from it.
6. Serve straight away.

Nutrition Value:

- Calories: 310 Cal
- Fat: 12 g
- Carbs: 50 g
- Protein: 2 g
- Fiber: 5 g

Mug Carrot Cake

Preparation time: 5 minutes
Cooking time: 15 minutes
Servings: 1

Ingredients:

- 2 tablespoons grated carrot
- 1/4 cups whole-wheat pastry flour
- 1/8 teaspoon ground dried ginger
- 2 tablespoons chopped walnuts
- 1/4 teaspoon baking powder
- 1 tablespoon coconut sugar
- 1/8 teaspoon salt
- 1/4 teaspoon ground cinnamon
- 1 tablespoons raisin
- 1/8 teaspoon ground allspice
- 2 tablespoons and 2 teaspoons almond milk
- 2 teaspoons olive oil

Method:

1. Switch on the air fryer, insert the fryer basket, then shut it with the lid, set the frying temperature 350 degrees F, and let it preheat for 5 minutes.
2. Meanwhile, take an ovenproof mug, place flour in it, stir in ginger, baking powder, salt, sugar, cinnamon, and allspice until mixed and then mix in carrots, raisins, nuts, oil, and milk until incorporated
3. Open the preheated fryer, place the prepared mug in it, close the lid and cook for 15 minutes until firm and a toothpick come out clean from the center of the cake.
4. When done, the air fryer will beep, then open the lid and take out the mug.
5. Serve straight away.

Nutrition Value:

- Calories: 168.6 Cal
- Fat: 11.5 g
- Carbs: 8.8 g
- Protein: 7.8 g
- Fiber: 1.5 g

Baked Apples

Preparation time: 5 minutes
Cooking time: 11 minutes
Servings: 4

Ingredients:

- 2 medium apples, cored
- 2 tablespoons coconut sugar
- 2/3 teaspoon ground cinnamon

Method:

1. Switch on the air fryer, insert the fryer basket, then shut it with the lid, set the frying temperature 360 degrees F, and let it preheat for 5 minutes.
2. Meanwhile, prepare the apples and for this, slice each apple lengthwise, and then remove the seeds.
3. Open the preheated fryer, place apples in it in a single layer, close the lid and cook for 10 minutes until tender.
4. Meanwhile, take a small bowl, stir together sugar and cinnamon in it, and set aside until required.
5. When done, the air fryer will beep, then open the lid, sprinkle sugar-cinnamon mixture on apples, shut with lid, and continue cooking for 1 minute.
6. When done, transfer apples to a dish and then serve.

Nutrition Value:

- Calories: 81 Cal
- Fat: 0 g
- Carbs: 22 g
- Protein: 0 g
- Fiber: 5 g

Donuts

Preparation time: 5 minutes
Cooking time: 18 minutes
Servings: 2

Ingredients:

- 3 cups cherries, pitted, halved
- 1/2 teaspoon almond extract, unsweetened
- 2 tablespoons maple syrup
- 4 tablespoons granola
- 1 tablespoon almond butter melted

Method:

1. Switch on the air fryer, insert the fryer basket, then shut it with the lid, set the frying temperature 350 degrees F, and let it preheat for 5 minutes.
2. Meanwhile, take a large ramekin, place cherries in it, and then stir in almond extract, butter and maple syrup until mixed.
3. Open the preheated fryer, place ramekin in it, close the lid and cook for 15 minutes until cooked, stirring halfway.
4. When done, the air fryer will beep, open the lid, top cherries with granola, and then continue cooking for 3 minutes until the top has turned brown.
5. Serve straight away.

Nutrition Value:

- Calories: 316 Cal
- Fat: 7 g
- Carbs: 62 g
- Protein: 4 g
- Fiber: 6 g

Peanut Butter Balls

Preparation time: 15 minutes
Cooking time: 20 minutes
Servings: 6

Ingredients:

- 1/2 cup coconut flour
- 2 tablespoons flaxseed
- 1/2 cup oats
- 1/2 teaspoon baking soda
- 1/3 cup maple syrup
- 1/2 teaspoon baking powder
- 1/2 cup peanut butter
- 5 tablespoons water, warmed

Method:

1. Prepare the flax egg and for this, place flax seeds a small bowl, stir in water until combined and let it stand for 5 minutes.
2. Then pour flax egg in a large bowl, add butter and maple syrup, whisk until smooth and then whisk in baking powder and soda until well combined.
3. Stir in oats and flour until incorporated and dough comes together, place the dough into the refrigerator for 10 minutes until chilled, and then shape the dough into twelve balls.
4. Meanwhile, switch on the air fryer, insert the fryer basket, then shut it with the lid, set the frying temperature 250 degrees F, and let it preheat for 5 minutes.
5. Open the preheated fryer, place balls in it in a single layer, close the lid and cook for 10 minutes until golden brown and cooked, shaking halfway.
6. When done, the air fryer will beep, then open the lid, and transfer balls to a dish.
7. Cook remaining balls in the same manner and then serve.

Nutrition Value:

- Calories: 97.8 Cal
- Fat: 5.5 g
- Carbs: 8.8 g
- Protein: 2.9 g
- Fiber: 1 g

Cinnamon Churros

Preparation time: 60 minutes
Cooking time: 25 minutes
Servings: 4

Ingredients:

For the Churros:

- 1 cup coconut flour
- 1/2 cup and 1 tablespoon coconut sugar
- 2 teaspoons cinnamon
- 1/2 teaspoon vanilla extract, unsweetened
- 1/2 cup almond butter
- 3 flax eggs
- 1 cup of water

For the Chocolate Sauce:

- 1 teaspoon coconut oil
- 3/4 cup chocolate chips, unsweetened

Method:

1. Prepare churros and for this, take a medium saucepan, place it over medium heat, pour in water and bring it to a boil.
2. Stir in butter and 1 tablespoon sugar, let it melts, switch heat to medium-low level and then fold in the flour until incorporated and the dough comes together, remove the pan from heat and set aside until required.
3. Take a medium bowl, place flax eggs in it and whisk in vanilla until combined.
4. Fold the flax egg mixture into the prepared dough until well combined and then let it stand for 15 minutes until cooked.
5. Transfer cooled dough into a piping bag with a star-shaped tip, take a baking pan, line it with parchment paper and pipe churros on it, about 6-inch long, and then chill them in the refrigerator for 30 minutes.
6. Meanwhile, switch on the air fryer, insert the fryer basket, then shut it with the lid, set the frying temperature 380 degrees F, and let it preheat.

7. Then open the preheated fryer, place churros in it in a single layer, close the lid and cook for 10 minutes until golden brown and cooked, shaking halfway.
8. Meanwhile, take a small bowl, place the cinnamon and remaining sugar in it and stir until mixed, set aside until required.
9. When done, the air fryer will beep, then open the lid, dredge churros into the cinnamon-sugar mixture, place them on a wire rack and cook remaining churros in the same manner.
10. In the meantime, prepare the chocolate sauce and for this, take a heatproof bowl, place chocolate chips in it, add oil and microwave for 30 seconds until chocolate has melted, and when done, stir well.
11. Dip churros into the chocolate sauce and serve.

Nutrition Value:

- Calories: 290 Cal
- Fat: 15 g
- Carbs: 37 g
- Protein: 3 g
- Fiber: 2 g

Stuffed and Spiced Baked Apples

Preparation time: 5 minutes
Cooking time: 10 minutes
Servings: 4

Ingredients:

- 1/3 cup rolled oats
- 4 medium apples
- 1/4 cup chopped pecans
- 1 teaspoon pumpkin spice seasoning
- 2 tablespoons raisins
- 1/4 cup maple syrup
- 2/3 cup water

Method:

1. Switch on the air fryer, insert the fryer basket, then shut it with the lid, set the frying temperature 340 degrees F, and let it preheat for 5 minutes.
2. Meanwhile, prepare the apples and for this, core them from the center but not all the way through the bottom and scoop out the seeds by using a spoon.
3. Take a medium bowl, place remaining ingredients in it, except for water, stir until mixed and stuff this mixture into the apples.
4. Take a shallow heatproof dish that fits into the air fryer, pour water in it, and place prepared apples in it.
5. Open the preheated fryer, place the dish containing apples in it, close the lid and cook for 15 minutes until fork-tender, turning and spraying with oil halfway.
6. When done, the air fryer will beep, then open the lid and take out the dish.
7. Serve straight away.

Nutrition Value:

- Calories: 178.4 Cal
- Fat: 4.3 g
- Carbs: 44.3 g
- Protein: 0.7 g
- Fiber: 4.9 g

Sweet Potato Dessert Fries

Preparation time: 5 minutes
Cooking time: 27 minutes
Servings: 2

Ingredients:

- 2 medium sweet potatoes, peeled
- 1/4 cup coconut sugar
- 1 tablespoon cornstarch
- 2 tablespoons cinnamon
- ½ tablespoon coconut oil
- Powdered sugar as needed for dusting

Method:

1. Switch on the air fryer, insert the fryer basket, then shut it with the lid, set the frying temperature 370 degrees F, and let it preheat for 5 minutes.
2. Meanwhile, cut peeled potatoes into ½-inch thick slices, place them in a bowl, add cornstarch and oil and toss until well coated.
3. Open the preheated fryer, place sweet potatoes in it in a single layer, close the lid, and cook for 18 minutes until golden brown and cooked, shaking halfway.
4. When all the fries have cooked, transfer them to a large bowl, sprinkle them with remaining coconut sugar and cinnamon and toss until coated.
5. Transfer potatoes to a dish, sprinkle with powdered sugar, and then serve.

Nutrition Value:

- Calories: 102.6 Cal
- Fat: 0.2 g
- Carbs: 23.6 g
- Protein: 2.3 g
- Fiber: 3.8 g

Donut Holes

Preparation time: 1 hour and 10 minutes
Cooking time: 12 minutes
Servings: 6

Ingredients:

- 1 cup almond flour
- 1 teaspoon baking powder
- 1/2 teaspoon salt
- 1/4 cup and 2 tablespoons coconut sugar, divided
- 2 1/4 teaspoons cinnamon, divided
- 1 tablespoon melted coconut oil
- 2 tablespoons chickpea liquid
- 1/4 cup soy milk

Method:

1. Take a large bowl, place flour in it, and stir baking powder, salt, ¼ cup sugar, and 2 teaspoons cinnamon in it.
2. Whisk in oil, milk and chickpea liquid until incorporated and the dough comes together and then chill it in the refrigerator for 1 hour.
3. Take a shallow dish, place remaining sugar and cinnamon in it and stir until mixed, set aside until required.
4. Switch on the air fryer, insert the fryer basket lined with parchment paper, then shut it with the lid, set the frying temperature 370 degrees F, and let it preheat for 5 minutes.
5. Meanwhile, remove chilled dough from the refrigerator, distribute it into twelve parts, shape each part into a ball and then dredge it with cinnamon-sugar mixture.
6. Open the preheated fryer, place balls in it in a single layer, spray with olive oil, close the lid and cook for 6 minutes until golden brown and cooked, don't shake.
7. When done, the air fryer will beep, then open the lid, transfer balls to a dish and let them cool completely.
8. Cook remaining donut balls in the same manner and then serve.

Nutrition Value:

- Calories: 190 Cal
- Fat: 9 g
- Carbs: 28 g
- Protein: 2 g
- Fiber: 1 g

Conclusion

There are many ways to achieve the objective of living a better life, and indeed, the plant-based diet has come out to be one of the effective ways. Mainly we struggle with self-control in the first few days on the plant-based diet, but with the help of smart decisions that can be made easy. With the advent of new technology, products have risen to help people eat healthier. One of these devices includes Air Fryer. An Air Fryer simply reduces the amount of oil consumption of a person using it significantly. Also, it does so by maintaining the texture and taste of its oil-fried version. It makes tasty plant-based meals with almost no compromise on taste-making the change towards a healthier life way easier.

Bon Apetit!

Made in the USA
Columbia, SC
21 January 2020